W9-APN-451

The Kentucky Bicentennial Bookshelf
Sponsored by

KENTUCKY HISTORICAL EVENTS CELEBRATION COMMISSION
KENTUCKY FEDERATION OF WOMEN'S CLUBS

and Contributing Sponsors

AMERICAN FEDERAL SAVINGS & LOAN ASSOCIATION
ARMCO STEEL CORPORATION, ASHLAND WORKS
A. ARNOLD & SON TRANSFER & STORAGE CO., INC. / ASHLAND OIL, INC.
BAILEY MINING COMPANY, BYPRO, KENTUCKY / BEGLEY DRUG COMPANY
J. WINSTON COLEMAN, JR. / CONVENIENT INDUSTRIES OF AMERICA, INC.
IN MEMORY OF MR. AND MRS. J. SHERMAN COOPER BY THEIR CHILDREN
CORNING GLASS WORKS FOUNDATION / MRS. CLORA CORRELL
THE COURIER-JOURNAL AND THE LOUISVILLE TIMES
COVINGTON TRUST & BANKING COMPANY
MR. AND MRS. GEORGE P. CROUNSE / GEORGE E. EVANS, JR.
FARMERS BANK & CAPITAL TRUST COMPANY / FISHER-PRICE TOYS, MURRAY
MARY PAULINE FOX, M.D., IN HONOR OF CHLOE GIFFORD
MARY A. HALL, M.D., IN HONOR OF PAT LEE,
JANICE HALL & MARY ANN FAULKNER
OSCAR HORNSBY INC. / OFFICE PRODUCTS DIVISION IBM CORPORATION
JERRY'S RESTAURANTS / ROBERT B. JEWELL
LEE S. JONES / KENTUCKIANA GIRL SCOUT COUNCIL
KENTUCKY BANKERS ASSOCIATION / KENTUCKY COAL ASSOCIATION, INC.
THE KENTUCKY JOCKEY CLUB, INC. / THE LEXINGTON WOMAN'S CLUB
LINCOLN INCOME LIFE INSURANCE COMPANY
LORILLARD A DIVISION OF LOEW'S THEATRES, INC.
METROPOLITAN WOMAN'S CLUB OF LEXINGTON / BETTY HAGGIN MOLLOY
MUTUAL FEDERAL SAVINGS & LOAN ASSOCIATION
NATIONAL INDUSTRIES, INC. / RAND MCNALLY & COMPANY
PHILIP MORRIS, INCORPORATED / MRS. VICTOR SAMS
SHELL OIL COMPANY, LOUISVILLE
SOUTH CENTRAL BELL TELEPHONE COMPANY
SOUTHERN BELLE DAIRY CO. INC.
STANDARD OIL COMPANY (KENTUCKY)
STANDARD PRINTING CO., H. M. KESSLER, PRESIDENT
STATE BANK & TRUST COMPANY, RICHMOND
THOMAS INDUSTRIES INC. / TIP TOP COAL CO., INC.
MARY L. WISS, M.D. / YOUNGER WOMAN'S CLUB OF ST. MATTHEWS

Cassius Marcellus Clay

Firebrand of Freedom

H. EDWARD RICHARDSON

THE UNIVERSITY PRESS OF KENTUCKY

Research for The Kentucky Bicentennial Bookshelf
is assisted by a grant from the
National Endowment for the Humanities.
Views expressed in the Bookshelf do not
necessarily represent those of the Endowment.

ISBN: 0-8131-0205-7

Library of Congress Catalog Card Number: 74-7882

Copyright © 1976 by The University Press of Kentucky

A statewide cooperative scholarly publishing agency
serving Berea College, Centre College of Kentucky,
Eastern Kentucky University, Georgetown College,
Kentucky Historical Society, Kentucky State University,
Morehead State University, Murray State University,
Northern Kentucky State College, Transylvania University,
University of Kentucky, University of Louisville, and
Western Kentucky University.

Editorial and Sales Offices: Lexington, Kentucky 40506

For Shawn Edward Richardson
& Jill Calvert Richardson

Contents

Preface

Cassius Marcellus Clay was a paradox in history. Born to wealth, he was an upholder of the oppressed. Clearly he was a man of intellect, and yet it was the passion of his words and actions that seared each central event of his life into the memories of his contemporaries. Though one of the great men of his age, he stood apart from all. Isolated and eccentric in his old age, he died to become an ageless legend, forever green in human memory.

Much of the meaning of Clay's life lay in its supreme individualism, inseparable elements of which were his personal style, his flair, his charisma—words that would have paled in abstraction beside the living man. Remembering Clay, Justice John M. Harlan wrote: "There is a more striking combination of manly beauty and strength in his face than in the face of any man whom I ever saw. I always had the highest regard for his integrity of character, his manliness, and his fidelity to his own convictions."

In this biographical essay I have endeavored above all else to avoid treating Clay as a Kentucky Quixote, on the one hand, or as a savior of the Union, on the other, although there is some truth in both views. Rather, I have endeavored to see Clay as his own records reveal him; at the same time I have attempted to view him in the setting of history and to present his life in a systematic narrative against that record of his times.

My research has led me to a view of Clay's life and career at variance with general opinion. Briefly stated, my contention is that his ideas were in principle consistent throughout his life. Certainly he intended from his early manhood to deal slavery a deathblow. But Clay was more than an emancipationist. He was committed to what he called "some great principle of human happiness"; before all things, Clay was a freedom hunter. His commitment to freedom of the press, for example, was as great as the martyred Lovejoy's.

Although Clay's letters, regrettably, are as yet uncollected, and further research remains to be done, I hope my efforts will throw light upon some previously obscure areas and correct some earlier misreadings of Clay's life. I hope also that this book will help Americans everywhere more aware of one of the nation's heroic figures.

While I have attempted to distinguish myth from fact, I have not thought it proper to ignore myth as it relates to Clay. Gilbert Murray describes the myth motif as "a strange, unanalyzed vibration below the surface, an undercurrent of desires and fears and passions, long slumbering yet eternally familiar." Though myths may seem "strange," there is yet "that within us which leaps at the sight of them, a cry of the blood which tells us we have known them always." In Clay's life, myth persists with such force that it reminds us, allowing for its exaggerations and distortions, that history, as La Rochefoucauld said, "never embraces more than a small part of reality."

My first knowledge of Clay goes back to the 1930s, to the Madison County Courthouse in Richmond, where I heard the few remaining Civil War veterans and their many admirers of all ages talk about him. I remember them well. They hitched up their splint-bottom chairs in the shade of August maples. Their barlow knives delicately pared cedar shavings that, like little wooden springs, danced to the ground. The older men could not negotiate such complicated whittling but rested their hands on the crooks of hickory canes. When the talk turned to "Cash" Clay, the whittling stopped. Knives and canes became punctuation marks as the old men grew eloquent. I remember their faces all aglow behind saffron-tinctured beards, their eyes burning under bushy white brows—a sudden excitement in the hot air.

"Rotten shame the fool killer didn't get around to 'Old Cash' before he died a natural death," they reckoned, "but he was a heller with a bowie knife." To them his public life was a crucible of volatile national issues, his private life a taunting outrage. Yet when the talk grew heated, when their faces shown hot as the isinglass of a roaring pot-bellied stove—and the most vehement critic was deep in bloody narrative, painting in exquisite detail the savage ferocity with which the old general defended his "damned principles"—invariably a strange undercurrent of awe, not unakin to admiration and envy, would sweep through those who remembered him.

For these reasons, I suppose, I do not recall a neutral statement ever made about him. Madison County was then overwhelmingly Democratic, and my mother was one of the few Republicans I knew. General Clay was a famous Republican, or if I were to believe those graybeards, an infamous Republican. In this community of traditional morality, General Clay's sins had found him out. He accumulated a wide range of colorful sobriquets: "old rip," and worse, "cradle-robber who bought dolls for his child bride to play with." And so on summer afternoons, the courthouse idlers recited their fathers' and grandfathers' denunciations of Clay as an "autocrat of hell." For nineteenth century proslavery Democrats this meant that he was, among other accomplishments, a Republican. Worse than that, he was a "black Republican"—often a "black-hearted rascal." "Black" was no simple metaphor: Old Cash had actually "voted the blacks." At Foxtown he had armed himself and marched "whole coffles, 60 or 80 at a time," to the polls.

People still argue about him, and some still hate him. It is not unusual even now to hear people say of him: "That old son of a bitch. He went against his time, against his own people." And that, as everyone in Madison County has always known, is the worst thing anyone can do.

So many people have assisted, directly and indirectly, in providing access to necessary sources and to a wealth of pertinent information that it seems proper that I direct the reader to both the "Addendum: The Russian Ballerina" and the "Note on Sources and Acknowledgments" at the end of this book. However, I wish to express my gratitude here to Mrs. Beulah Nunn, who, with the cooperation of General Clay's descendants, and hundreds of interested people throughout Kentucky and the country, brought White Hall from dilapidation to enduring monument and state shrine. Indeed hers is an achievement for which all Kentuckians will be forever grateful.

I am indebted to Dr. Sydney Schultze for her advice and research in Russian sources; to Sharon Sullivan Long and Jeanne Paschal, who typed the manuscript; to Dr. David W. Maurer and Dr. Leon V. Driskell, who read portions of the manuscript; to Elizabeth Bell for proofreading; and to my wife, Antonia Calvert Richardson, who once again provided invaluable stenographic aid and critical insights.

In the 1960s I first began talking over my ideas for a book on her great-grandfather with Miss Esther Bennett of Richmond, Kentucky. I wish to express my thanks for her permission to use the prints of the Frazer portrait of the young Clay, of the G. P. A. Healey painting of the young Mary Jane Clay, and of the Brady imperial mezzotint of the middle-aged Clay. Thanks are also due her for much valuable information on White Hall—for arranging my visits to the mansion before it became a state shrine, for the use of other photographs in her possession, and for providing me access to her helpful correspondence on White Hall, including her letter from Clay Lancaster, July 12, 1967, containing his definitive essay, "The Architecture of White Hall," my source for detailed architectural references. For those many hours of enlightenment and encouragement I spent with Miss Bennett, I shall always be obliged—so much so that this formal acknowledgment seems inadequate, and this expression of gratitude, though genuine, but a lame sentiment.

1

DAWN AT WHITE HALL

Between Richmond and Lexington in the Bluegrass, in the upland meadows above the palisades of the Kentucky River, looms White Hall. It was built to impress by the sheer grandeur of its high spaciousness and ornamentation and to express a personality worthy of its towering conception. Major Thomas Lewinski, who came to Lexington from the University of Louisville in 1842, conceived the design, and John McMurtry of Lexington executed it during the 1860s.

People for miles around identify this landmark as the Cassius Marcellus Clay homeplace.

Out of all his landholdings surveyed from Ohio to the Mississippi River, Green Clay, a pioneer from Powhatan County, Virginia, chose an eminence in Madison County, with its gently undulating hills and rich, productive soil, for his estate. The original log cabin on the site dated back to the 1780s and Green Clay's trusteeship of Boonesborough. The imposing Victorian mansion seen there today wraps around the eastern and northern sides of the older Georgian structure, "Clermont"—a two-story dwelling of brick, laid in Flemish bond, with heavy rangework of Kentucky marble and gray limestone, which Green Clay built in 1798–1799. In this eighteenth-century house, now a rear appendage of the mansion but carefully preserved intact, Cassius Marcellus Clay was

1

born October 19, 1810; he was General Green Clay's third son, the youngest of six children.

The forebears of Cassius Clay on both sides had come to America before the Revolutionary War. His mother, Sally Lewis, was the granddaughter of Edward Payne of Virginia, who, Collins notes in his *History of Kentucky* (1847), "struck General Washington for an insult, for which that great man promptly and magnanimously apologized, and Payne was ever after one of his most devoted admirers and friends." Cassius Clay's father was a hero of the War of 1812, as well as a Kentucky pioneer.

Clay's life swept a century when American society was on the brink of huge transformations. A new sense of freedom to seek, of adventure, made the dawn of each day electric with hope. The Industrial Revolution, the Monroe Doctrine, Henry Clay's American System, and the Missouri Compromise seemed to promise that the good of the new world would triumph over the evil of the old. The French and American revolutions had inspired a romantic age springing from Wordsworth, Byron, and Keats, and reaching to Emerson, Melville, and Whitman. For Coleridge musing in dejection, America was a "green light that lingers in the west." Energies unknown since the Renaissance fired flames of optimism. The flourishing new democracy prospered as effete old-world autocracies shrank. The perfectibility of the common man became a living experiment. Altruism, philanthropy, and reform quickened the very air. But the contradiction of slavery in the American republic prefigured great crises of national disunity: sectionalism, the Civil War, the assassination of Lincoln, and then the divisive Reconstruction politics by which, Cassius Clay lamented, "the South was finally made solid," bringing to grief the old Republican party he had helped to found.

Clay was an instrument in many of the events that spanned the history of America from Jacksonian Democracy to the controversial election of Rutherford B. Hayes in 1876. The subsequent withdrawal of Federal troops from the southern states, in Clay's view, restored them to their original equal autonomy and thus restored also the Union in which he believed. Then, as he approached his seventies, Clay left the political wars and returned to White Hall. A decade later, determined not to be forgotten, he struck the epigraph of his *Memoirs* (1886) in flaring Latin: *"Quorum—pars fui."* [*"Of them—I was a part."*]

Clay's later years most trouble historians and biographers. The best they can do is to declare that the old patriot "lived too long." Concerning his old age, Clay's literary executor wrote in the preface of Clay's personal revisions of his *Memoirs* (1886), "When the eagle begins to lose his plumage with age, he withdraws to a home on the solitary tower or mountain crag, and there lives, in serene dignity and imperial pride, with memories of the allurements and rapture of the conflict, and the blazonry of a triumphant career."

The nineteenth century passed into the twentieth. Then, for decades, White Hall was left to tenant farmers, even to their chickens and pigs, abandoned finally to tramps, vandals, casual intruders, and passing lovers who left behind them crude mementos—a burnt-out fire on the ballroom floor, empty bottles, and a thousand graffiti scratched into the white plaster walls and Corinthian columns. But even as the house went to rack and ruin, it retained its legend. It was the habitation of a man no longer mortal, often likened to a lion: his imperial presence animated the high-ceilinged rooms and in troubled isolation prowled the corridors.

Now White Hall is restored to its original lustre. Sconces and chandeliers burn in bright repudiation of the dark years of neglect. In the late afternoon, those steeped in its lore are sometimes struck with the strange illusion that White Hall is as much spirit as brick and mortar. Remote as another century, persistent as summer thunder, it thrusts itself up, courageous and a little ab-

3

surd, too, shouldering its way into the frail golden grandeur of a dying sun. Through the rooms of the state shrine, young women in nineteenth-century dress conduct the visitors, evoking romantic moods with a brace of dueling pistols in a rosewood case, a bowie knife under glass, a bewitching portrait of a mysteriously seductive lady: "A friend of General Clay," one may be told. "We think she was a famous Russian ballerina."

And the tour moves on. The Lion's presence, though vaguely felt, eludes both guide and tourist.

2

INTIMATIONS

HIS FIRST COMMON school was hardly more than an adventure in the woods, where an unchinked log cabin stood less than a mile from White Hall. Sally Lewis Clay, like most mothers, was reluctant to see him leave home. But he would not be afraid, he assured her, even if his brother Brutus, two years his senior, were not going with him. And so they set out through the grapevine-hung forest, their book satchels slung over their shoulders, carrying the lunch basket by turns.

In summer they would take off the hated shoes and socks and wade in the rain puddles and rivulets that fed a tributary of Tate's Creek. Leaving his books on the puncheon log bench, Cassius raced through the cool water, his feet flinging silver spears from his path. At lunch he and Brutus treated themselves to the daily feasts with which their mother had filled the lunch basket—topped off with the "A B C" mystery. What would it be today? "A" for fried apple turnovers in the shape of half-moons! "B" for beaten biscuits, halved with thick, tender wedges of hickory-cured ham! "C" for the fresh cherry preserves made from the same basketful he had picked the Saturday before in the south orchard. He had turned the crank of the cherrystoner himself.

Strong and quick, Cassius had a way of being in the center of things. The neighborhood girls laughed and removed their homespun stockings, too, and splashed him with the cool waters at playtime.

His first real fight was with an overseer's son. Cassius mastered him and gave him a badly scratched face in the process. The boy's mother complained to Sally Lewis Clay, who sternly summoned Cassius to the house. There he was met by his mother, who had a peach-tree rod ready and did not spare it. But this was not to be the last of his fights.

From his mother Cassius learned that truth was the basis of all moral character. She could not tolerate even conventional lies and would never allow family or servants to tell callers that she was not at home when she was. "Beg them to excuse me," she would say instead. In such an atmosphere the boy developed a powerful respect for even commonplace honesty, although it required a more direct lesson as well. On one occasion, having clothed a lie in the "velvet vestments of a story," the boy found himself being summoned unmistakably for another whipping. But this time he took to his heels and ran.

He should have known better. His mother was a Calvinist Baptist, firm of purpose and not one to trifle with. She went relentlessly after him and soon had all the kitchen servants joining the pursuit. Cassius took his stand upon "a pile of stone-siftings," picked up rocks, and made things lively for the servants. "For," he declared, "as I had been whipped for fighting, now I fought not to be whipped." Finally, his mother had to come to him herself. She stood in solemn censure and looked up at him. The boy dropped his stones and submitted to the second and last whipping of his life. "Thank God," he wrote years later of his mother, "I never in childhood even raised my hand or turned my heart against her."

General Green Clay was the boy's hero. One of Cassius's earliest memories was of that colorful panoply —"the brilliant buttons and plumes" of the 3,000 Kentucky volunteers led by his father to the relief of Fort Meigs during the War of 1812. The boy had heard the story of his father's cutting his way through enemy lines to the fort and then successfully defending it against double odds—the combined 1,500 British troops under General Proctor and 5,000 Indians under the famed Tecumseh. He also knew that his father was one of the wealthiest landowners in the West, having surveyed at great danger to himself tens of thousands of acres of land from Ohio and the Bluegrass south to the region below the Tennessee River, claiming ownership of half the lands he surveyed.

But as a boy, Cassius saw little of his father. More often than not Green Clay was absent from White Hall, and when he was at home he was usually absorbed in business. The young Benjamin of the family often endeavored to gain his father's attention.

On one occasion, Green Clay tied a newly purchased Merino ram to a tree and went in to dinner. Cassius began to tease the skittish animal. It stamped its front hooves into the earth, lowered its head, and charged him to the end of its rope—which jerked it back again, like a buggy whip snapping itself in the air. If the boy was indeed seeking the attention of his father, he could not have succeeded more fully in getting it: he was in the act of inviting a trial of hardness of heads with the ram when Green Clay, returning and seeing his son's danger, rushed up and with the flat of his hand knocked Cassius farther than the sheep could have done. Later in life, Clay was fond of relating how some of his enemies, upon hearing the story, maintained that his father had taken needless precautions, "for my head would have proved too hard for the buck."

Still, it was the only time his father ever struck him a physical blow; Green Clay preferred to instruct his son through homely apothegms and firsthand experience. When Cassius was twelve or thirteen years old, the general sent him on horseback to Cincinnati to pay taxes on some land he owned in Ohio. The money was sewn into the boy's clothes, and he had a long-bladed pocketknife for defense. Once he had passed Lexington to the north, his trip led him through a lonely region of sparsely settled forests; after he reached Cincinnati, he faced a different kind of threat.

Cassius was old enough to be alert to danger but not mature enough to suspect what shape it would take or to know how to meet it. In Cincinnati he was hoodwinked by a Dickensian character called Birdseye, who, after gaining the youth's confidence with a guise of piety and friendship, tricked him into revealing the purpose of his trip. Then with an accomplice Birdseye attempted to waylay him at night near the creaking wharves of the river town. Sensing his danger, however, Cassius eluded the trap set for him and, with the native sagacity of a farm boy who knows his directions, managed to get back to the safety of his hotel.

He paid the taxes and returned home, but as he rode he began in good earnest to put Green Clay's maxims into practice. He allowed no horseman to be with him long on the road. He either galloped forward or reined his mount back until he was alone. The lesson had taught him suspicion, and he refused ever after to go about cities with strangers. As the common school had been an exercise in nature rather than letters, the business journey to Cincinnati had become a course in self-reliance, a dramatic illustration of his father's apothegm, "Never tell anyone your business."

Other adages, too, were engraved upon his mind: "Enquire of fools and children, if you wish to get at the truth." "Never set your name on the right-hand side of the writing." "Never say of anybody what you would not have proclaimed in the courthouse yard." "Well is the tongue called a two-edged sword, for it makes irreparable feuds." "A man will forgive an injury before an insult."

And as he was later to have more occasion than one to remember, "When traveling in dangerous times, never return by the same road."

After attending Madison Academy in Richmond, Cassius and Brutus were tutored in the home of Joshua Fry on the Dix River in Garrard County. A man of private fortune, Fry was a celebrated teacher who amused himself by indulging his scholarly whims—teaching his own grandchildren and a few selected pupils from wealthy families in the Bluegrass. Here Cassius learned to read Caesar's *Gallic Wars*, Cicero's orations, and Virgil's *Aeneid* from a master Latinist.

Both Cassius and Brutus followed Fry to Danville, where he continued to teach Latin at Centre College. They lived with Joshua Fry's son, Thomas, and shared a pleasant life with the Virginia family. Cassius loved to fish in the crystal riffles of the river for bass and perch. Like other romantics of his generation, Cassius believed that he gained not only pleasure but also strength from the earth. In communion with nature, he wrote, "the body and soul are made robust for the great trials of life." In the evenings the young men and women danced the Virginia reel to the accompaniment of their host's violin. Life with the Joshua Fry family was an experience the Clay boys would ever remember—a school in manners as well as in academics.

After Cassius and Brutus had completed their studies in Latin and other branches of learning—rhetoric, the classics, and philosophy—the amiable Brutus went into business in Bourbon County as a farmer and stock producer. Much like Green Clay in ability and habits, he was well suited to the life of a Bluegrass landowner and in time became eminently successful.

But in his thirteenth year Cassius was sent to Saint Joseph's College in Bardstown, where he joined nearly two hundred other students from all over the South. Saint Joseph's, the oldest Catholic college in Kentucky, was

9

founded by Bishop Benedict J. Flaget in 1819. By 1825 the school boasted a spacious four-story brick building; and during the years in which Cassius Clay leisurely studied the international language of diplomacy with the Frenchman Priest Fouché, it was filled to capacity. Cassius boarded with William Elder, the father of the president of the college.

It was here that he learned to savor the delicacy of frogs' legs. And it was here that he had another fight. Just after the supervising priest had stepped outside, a classroom bully provoked a small boy into an outburst of tears; the child was too small to reach his tormentor, although he tried. As Cassius watched the unfair encounter, a red rage fired all he saw. Suddenly he sprang upon a bench, just above the height of the big boy. When the startled Hector turned, Cassius hit him a stinging blow upon the nose. The blood flew in all directions and the bully backed off, utterly confounded. Just then the priest looked in and, observing the situation, went out again, affecting to have seen nothing.

The alumni roster at Saint Joseph's College includes the names of Theodore O'Hara, the poet; Jefferson Davis; James Speed, who became Lincoln's attorney general; and several governors. Cassius visited with the leading families of Nelson County, including the Rowans of Federal Hill. He also knew Rowan and James Hardin, as well as their father, Benjamin, and visited the family at their imposing new colonial brick mansion, Edgewood, in Bardstown. While at Saint Joseph's, at his father's suggestion Cassius began a correspondence in French with his cousin Henry Clay, then secretary of state under John Quincy Adams. He enjoyed the advantages of conversation with the Spanish-American students and with the French Catholics from Louisiana. But the greatest lesson learned at Saint Joseph's, in his own judgment, was that of being "ever tolerant in religion."

Although he had been quick to fight, he soon perceived

the example of his father, who was shrewd enough to avoid unnecessary conflicts. He remembered a story his father had told years before about a man who owed him money and, instead of paying his debt, had tried to badger him with a challenge. But Green Clay replied that if the man "would pay him first, he would fight him afterward." In the mind of the youngest son, Green Clay's prudence in no way diluted his bravery and in this instance "settled the question, of course, without a fight."

Sally Clay was, in accordance with her Baptist principles, a teetotaler. Yet much of the enormous grain harvest of White Hall was sent to the family distilleries in Madison and Fayette counties to be made into whiskey. Barrels of the liquid cargo were hauled to various taverns and stagecoach stops in the Bluegrass, as well as to Clay's Ferry for shipment downriver, where it found a ready market at many points along the Kentucky, the Ohio, and the Mississippi.

Green Clay was not a Calvinist Baptist; he was a Deist. Yet he gave strong lip service to his wife's condemnation of corn liquor—especially, Cassius observed, when she was within earshot. Each morning for years Cassius watched his father take his bourbon tonic, usually before breakfast. Ceremonially, his father would go to the buffet and lift from it his old Virginia military wine chest, which contained about a half dozen cups and as many square English bottles of very thin glass, finely inlaid with goldleaf. From one bottle, filled with bitter camomile flowers and native bourbon, the general would pour a glass of whiskey. He would make a rueful face at Cassius and the others, then bravely swallow the hated liquid. Sometimes Cassius saw his mother roll her eyes ceilingward; for a long time he thought she could not bear to see his father's silent suffering. Yet the boy could not get it clear in his mind why "if it was good for papa, it was not good for us."

Overwhelmed with curiosity, Cassius one day decided

11

to experiment with the bitter libation, modeling his procedure on that of the general. Swallowing the liquor, he prepared to screw up his face as Green Clay always did, but he discovered that he was not really suffering. "I found it very far from bitter," he remembered, "and the camomile was but a sham."

His father was one of the most prominent slaveholders in the West, and from earliest childhood the boy was aware of slavery. But he had no aversion to it, for at White Hall, as Clay wrote many years later, slavery was made "as bearable as was consistent with the facts." Green Clay provided his slaves with "first-class clothing, food, and shelter." An incident of Cassius's childhood, however, awakened the boy to the darker meaning of slavery.

Mary, a comely mulatto girl of about eighteen who was a flower gardener at White Hall, helped Cassius and his sister make a miniature garden, and the children grew fond of her. Later, as a temporary arrangement, Mary was sent by General Clay to work in the house of one of the overseers. One day Cassius and Eliza, standing in their little garden, heard a piercing scream; it was Mary, coming into the yard. To the horror of all, she held a butcher knife in front of her, and her clothes were drenched with blood. The servants ran wildly from the fields and cabins and surrounded her, crying out with her in a communion of fear.

Cassius later came to understand that Payne, the drunken overseer, had attacked her. In self-defense she killed him with the knife, and then ran back to White Hall. Mary was taken to jail, later to be tried and acquitted. Nevertheless, in accordance with the custom of Kentucky and the other border slave states of that time, she was ordered to be sent into the Deep South. The innocence—the indifference—with which Cassius had viewed slavery was swept away. Years later he wrote:

Never shall I forget—and through all these years it rests upon the memory as the stamp upon a bright coin—the scene, when

Mary was tied by the wrists and sent from home and friends, and the loved features of her native land—the home of her infancy and girlish days—into Southern banishment forever; and yet held guiltless by a jury of, not her "peers," but her oppressors! Never shall I forget those . . . faces—the oppressor and the oppressed, rigid with equal agony! She cast an imploring look at me, as if in appeal; but meekly went, without a word, as "a sheep to the slaughter."

The eloquent language of Robert J. Breckinridge echoed his own dawning emancipationism: "The greatest of all rights is the right of a man to himself." But slavery seemed the fixed order of things.

The Richmond girl who was the brightest light of Clay's youth remains mysteriously nameless. He refers to her as "E.R.——," and she was the first woman of this romantic young student's world. Just younger than he, she had long blonde hair; "To see her was to love her," he said later. Inspired by her beauty, Cassius wrote and published a poem, "Lines," the romantic persona of which eschews the wisdom of the Magi and instead quests for a "woman's eyes" to look upon. His "spirit" wanders the "Lybian wilds." Although it has drunk "a thousand smiles," it "yet thirsts again." This persona is Prometheus, too, the fabled one upon whose entrails the vultures prey: "My heart . . ./Though long by passion fed upon,/Wastes not away."

Impulsively, Clay began to think of marriage. But the lovers' passions attracted attention, and they were subjected to jealous eyes, questioning, and gossip—what Clay called "vulgar espionage and offensive comments." The young lady's family suddenly left Richmond, never to return.

In his confusion, the boy-man's first thought was to follow her and avow his passion, thus proving "the sincerity of the tacit promise." But ardent though he was, he was too young not to be too proud to take this step. As an old man he spoke of his vivid memory of his first love: "Thus perished, as with one awaking, a beautiful dream; but its memory remains forever! . . . one undissoluble tie of kindred souls, which fill with sunshine or shade all after-life."

The pangs of first love, commencing with his later years at Saint Joseph's College, reveal a complex of emotions. Troubled as they were, these days were later perceived as part of a halcyon past, possibly because a deeper tragedy awaited the youth. He learned that his seventy-one-year-old father was dying of cancer.

For months after leaving Bardstown in April 1828, Cassius nursed the old general, who represented all that young Clay admired in the pioneer America of the preceding century. For months Green Clay watched, in John Quincy Adams's dying phrase, "the last of earth" pass before him. "Without the tremor of a nerve," as his youngest son observed, he stoically prepared his business papers, spent the weeks with his wife and son, and arranged his will in such a way that White Hall would be entailed to eighteen-year-old Cassius, along with over 2,200 acres, 17 slaves, and his portion of about 50,000 acres below the Tennessee River.

Only once was the old general's mind disturbed. The evening before his death, October 31, 1828, he called Cassius to his bedside and pointed northward, beyond the penumbra of the flickering candles in the direction of the family graveyard, where his body still lies. He spoke his last words to his dearest son: "I have just seen death come in at that door."

3

A LIGHT ON THE ROAD

A FEW MILES from White Hall a steep cliff towers above the Kentucky River, where banks of stratified limestone form a 200-foot crest. Once young Clay, struggling with a purebred bull, exploded in a blind fury and ran the bull over the precipice. "That bull has gone to hell," he told a neighbor. And so the name of the high point on the Kentucky River remains "Bull's Hell." But such violence could have been only a temporary relief from the aching emptiness.

He roamed the grounds of White Hall and spent hours in the library. Clay's was a generation in thrall to the great Romantics—Wordsworth, Coleridge, Byron, Shelley, and Keats. Small wonder that his introduction to death—"that greatest of calamities," as he later wrote of these hours of woe—stirred the young reader so deeply. Having fallen under the particular spell of Byron, Cassius cried, *"Oh Ada, death has come into the world!"*

Soon after his father's death in 1828, Clay entered Transylvania University. Founded in 1780, Transylvania was the oldest university west of the Alleghenies and was the cultural center of Lexington, already known for a generation as the Athens of the West.

Although he took classes in a wide range of subjects, he joined a philosophical society and pursued oratory as his major interest. At this time he began to study the great political issues and the great men who debated them. He must have remembered with gratitude his father's urging him to write Henry Clay from Saint Joseph's over a year before. Now he observed the master of Ashland, only recently secretary of state, in the very act of mending his fences at home while his popular opponent Andrew Jackson assumed the presidency in Washington. He heard the distinguished Presbyterian minister, Robert J. Breckinridge, advocate the gradual emancipation of slaves, while the "Old Duke," Robert Wickliffe, Sr., vigorously opposed him. One of Clay's classmates was Montgomery Blair, who later served in Lincoln's cabinet. Among his friends were also Robert "Young Duke" Wickliffe, Jr.; James Clay, the son of Henry; and James S. Rollins, later to be congressman from Missouri.

Lexington was then the center of wealth and refinement in Kentucky, Louisville and Covington being but small towns. The fine old courthouse at Main and Cheapside, surrounded with professional offices, businesses, and the shops of artisans, was the hub of official and commercial activities. A reporter of the *Western Monthly Magazine* noted the quiet streets of the residential areas, the old mansions shaded with venerable trees, the unostentatious beauty of the new edifices, and their individuality, which arose out of taste and dignity. He was also taken with the unusual number of pleasure carriages—gigs, barouches, coaches—that dashed along the streets in the cool of the late afternoons. Such establishments as Monsieur Mathurin Giron's Confectionery and Saloon on Mill Street attracted fashionable citizens of means, young and old, who wished to sample the Swiss cook's famed pastries or dance at soirées under the high frescoed ceilings of its ballrooms.

As a student, Clay visited and for a time lived with the Robert S. Todd family, close friends of his parents, at their home on West Short Street. He also called on them after they had moved to their Georgian colonial house, erected by house-joiner Mathias Shryock, at 574 West Main Street. Mary Ann Todd was barely thirteen at that time, but she and Cassius became good friends.

It was the daughter of a member of the medical school faculty, Dr. Elisha Warfield, who caught his eye. She was seventeen and Clay twenty when they first met. Having called at the Warfield home, Cassius and the other guests sat talking "in some constraint" during afternoon reception hours. Mary Jane, returning from one of Lexington's female academies, bolted in, dropping her sunbonnet on the anteroom couch and tossing her satchel of books in a chair. Dressed in "plain, but loosecut school-girl's attire" as Cassius remembered her, she had the "gay, fascinating manners, which are so noted in Irish women." Mary Jane entered at once into the conversation and soon had the attention of all the visitors. She seemed especially to enjoy Cassius Clay's admiration.

His reaction to Mary Jane Warfield suggests sudden recognition rather than considered discovery. Her eyes were a light grayish blue, large and far apart, "with that flexibility of iris which gives always great variety and intensity of expression." Again, his description of her somewhat "large mouth" with "flexible lips," and the light auburn of her hair, tinged with "nut-color, long and luxuriant" suggests illusion as much as reality. Doubtless he saw her at other places in Lexington—perhaps at Monsieur Giron's, at the races at the new Kentucky Association track, with her family as they rode by in an open carriage, or during social evenings at one of the fine old homes in Lexington or its environs. He called again at her home also. Just before he left Lexington to explore the advantages of the East in 1831, he presented her with Washington Irving's *Sketch Book*.

Inscribed on the blank leaves, naturally enough, were a few lines from Byron.

Upon arriving in Boston, Clay briefly considered the educational prospects of Harvard but decided on Yale instead. Although he stated that the scholastic reputation

of the New Haven university was "a prime quality . . . with me," he based his final decision on the beauty
of the trees in the Old Yard of the Yale campus. He wrote
to his brother Brutus that he would make it his business
"to examine men" rather than buildings, museums, and
what he termed "inanimate curiosities." Like a young
James Boswell (whose work he admired), Clay in his
travels of that year vigorously sought and secured interviews with great men in all walks of life. As a Henry Clay
Whig, he did not expect the friendly reception he received from President Jackson, whom he remembered as
a man of striking presence, over six feet in height, with a
fine build and military carriage. His clipped gray hair
stood up erect, like the man, and his head was "high and
expansive." Though an enemy of Henry Clay, to young
Cassius the president was "courteous, affable, and agreeable as possible." Above all, the young man was impressed with Old Hickory's "moral courage."

Clay dined with Martin Van Buren and met his family.
Noting Van Buren's rather square German face and head,
Clay found him "kind but reserved," a manner which
struck him as distinctively northern—not just different
but totally removed from the warm social intercourse of
the South. In Philadelphia, he met John Sargent, too, and
the Ingersoll and Biddle families.

Clay also became acquainted with Daniel Webster, and
at a ball at his house was awed by the largest private
library he had ever seen. He remembered the "massive,
high forehead, and distinguished bearing" of George
Ticknor and encountered many other distinguished men
and women of Boston, among them John Greenleaf Whit-
tier, Julia Ward Howe, Edward Everett, and Charles
Sumner. Although he was not presented to him, he saw
Rufus Choate, the lawyer, and never forgot his large frame
and great thoughtful eyes.

One of Clay's letters from Yale to his brother Brutus,
dated December 1831, emphasizes his continuing interest in travel and public affairs. He was becoming con-

vinced that he should enter politics. With that determination, maturity rapidly followed; Clay informed his brother that he had been at the books long enough to make any man "an artificial if not a natural fool." Still, he would not be hasty; his heeding of "prudence and necessity" in choosing the course of his life upon his return to Kentucky revealed his coming of age. It is in this context that his comments on the institution of slavery take on special importance: "But the time is coming when you as well as myself will have to put into requisition all the real power of understanding and firmness, which either of us may have to boast. The slave question is now assuming an importance in the opinions of the enlightened and humane, which prejudice and interest cannot long withstand. The slaves of Virginia, Kentucky and in fact all the slave holding states must soon be free!"

Clay marveled at the wealth about him in a land, not of rich bluegrass, but of "wooden nutmegs and leather pumpkin seed," as he derided its agricultural merits in order to celebrate by contrast its free working class. Here self-sufficiency and education were the rule rather than the exception. Industrial wealth not only enriched the few but provided jobs for the many, who in turn became customers for small tradesmen and made the growing towns prosperous. Signs of poverty were rare in comparison to those of Clay's own region. Moreover, tax monies were available for internal improvements. Thus Clay came gradually to believe that human bondage, denounced throughout the North as the besetting evil of the South, was neither practical nor rational. Clay would not quarrel with the moral grounds that made Thomas Jefferson tremble for his country when he reflected that God was just; but the young Kentuckian's earliest opposition to slavery was based primarily on his economic theories, which were largely those of the Henry Clay Whigs.

Although slavery-based agriculture was undoubtedly profitable, Clay and other Henry Clay Whigs saw the future of Kentucky and the nation in terms of Henry

Clay's American System. Through his cousin's influence, Clay came to believe that all parts of the nation needed free and educated workers, a balance of factories and agriculture, internal improvements such as roads and schools, a strong national bank to handle the government's financial business, and a protective tariff to encourage domestic manufactures. With the American System, as Clay perceived it, slavery was inconsonant.

Though the viewpoint of northern abolitionists was later to influence his attitudes toward slavery, Clay was by no means ready to embrace their political principles. Such men as William E. Channing and William H. Seward were to declare, "There is a higher law than the Constitution," but that position struck Clay as narrow and unrealistic. Behind him was the tradition of Jefferson, Washington, and other eighteenth-century liberals of the South who had hated slavery but feared that economic and racial upheavals and a crisis in national unity would follow liberation. They had advocated education of slaves and gradual emancipation according to the laws of each state and the Constitution of the United States. Of profound concern to the national leaders a generation later—Henry Clay and John C. Calhoun foremost among them—was the ever-pressing need of mediation between diverse, competing regions of the country. Only with unity, they believed, could the young nation develop its resources, break forever with its colonial past, and move toward that destined hegemony in the western hemisphere of which each patriot dreamed.

Henry Clay, though a slaveholder, was known as a gradual emancipationist and served as president of the American Colonization Society. He would oppose abolition in 1842, shortly before his canvass against southern Democrat James K. Polk, indicating the movement as "a delusion" that "arrays state against state." But in a letter of 1849, the Great Commoner was to outline a plan that would result in emancipation of all slaves in the course of about a generation and called for expatriation of free blacks—objectives favored by most antislavery Whigs.

Shortly before Cassius enrolled at Yale, he and his eldest brother, Princeton-educated Sidney P. Clay, had agreed to free their slaves and joined an emancipation society in Mercer County. Their action reflects the moral concerns of many New England Calvinists, who by 1830 had been swept with religious revivals unequaled in their fervor and were channeling their enthusiasms into such dynamic reform movements as abolition. "I felt all the horrors of slavery," Clay asserted. His childhood memory of Mary, acquitted by a jury of her oppressors and yet sent into southern exile, remained for him an epitome of those horrors. "But my parents were slave-holders; and I regarded it as I did other evils of humanity, as the fixed law of Nature or of God, and submitted as best I might."

Two of Clay's closest friends at Yale were Allen T. Caperton of Virginia, the class clown, who later became senator of both the Confederacy and the restored Union; and philanthropist Joseph Longworth of Cincinnati, then a student of "decidedly literary" tastes. Perhaps it was the latter who called Clay's attention to a scheduled speech of William Lloyd Garrison, printer and editor of the inflammatory new *Liberator*. The first number appeared in January 1831, advocating immediate abolition. "Urge me not to moderation in a cause like the present," Garrison wrote. "I am in earnest—I will not equivocate—I will not excuse—I will not retreat a single inch—AND I WILL BE HEARD."

"Who is Garrison?" Clay asked.

"Why, Garrison is the Abolitionist," he was told. "Don't you know?"

Clay decided to learn, and so went to South Church and heard Garrison. The experience was, in his own words, a "new revelation." In a lucid and logical speech, Garrison treated the "Divine Institution," as Clay wrote, "so as to burn like a branding-iron into the most callous hide of the slave-holder and his defenders." Garrison's arguments and sentiments were to him "as water to a thirsty wayfarer."

Clay's reaction strikes one as an anticipation of Walt Whitman's hymn of self-discovery—"Now in a moment I know what I am for." The very violence of the imagery with which he described his experience foreshadowed the course of Clay's life: "Garrison dragged out the monster from his citadels, and left him stabbed to the vitals, and dying at the feet of every logical and honest mind."

Clay believed that the "good seed which Garrison had watered, and which my own bitter experience had sown, aroused my whole soul." During his senior year his emotions were stirred at a revival and he was baptized in New Haven Sound by a Baptist minister. But he found his religious views in direct conflict with those of the cold, technical, and dogmatic churchmen, both Calvinist Baptist and Presbyterian, who were defenders of slavery even in New Haven. Upon returning to the Bluegrass, he wrote to the New Haven minister to strike his name from the church roll. Anticipating Mark Twain's Huck Finn, who maintained that he would "go to hell" rather than send "Nigger Jim" back into slavery, Clay said, "I preferred, if God was on that side, to stand with the Devil rather; for he was *silent*, at least."

Clay's antislavery convictions were distinctive. Although he could be an ally of such abolitionists as Garrison, he was not one of them. Like them he believed in agitating the question of slavery, but not only because he wished to deliver a deathblow to human bondage: he believed that the slaveholding class was making other assaults on freedom aside from holding men as chattels, and like John Quincy Adams he passionately opposed abrogations of constitutional guarantees.

Garrison, on the other hand, even in his tribute to the murdered abolitionist Elijah P. Lovejoy, killed by a mob while defending his life and his press at Alton, Illinois, in 1837, criticized the martyr for failing to practice "non-resistance." Garrison also disapproved of abolitionists who took part in political action. Refusing to recognize a government that sanctioned slavery, he ignored all constitutional means for achieving freedom of the blacks. At Yale and afterward Clay stood by the Constitution, "the supreme law" of the land. He would fight slavery under it, to be sure, but he would also fight to defend it, and he would use it in any way he could to survive the fight and to promote human happiness. Just as he had little sympathy for Hayne, who spoke of "Liberty first and Union afterwards," he dissented from Garrison, who by 1854 would have publicly burned a copy of the Constitution, dramatically crying out, "So perish all compromisers with tyranny!"

Clay was graduated with honors and chosen by his class to deliver an address in commemoration of the Washington Centennial, February 22, 1832. In the florid oratorical style of the day, he rejoiced in the patriotic moment, and then directed his first antislavery remarks to a large, distinguished audience: "Does no painful reflection rush across the unquiet conscience? no blush of insincerity suffuse the countenance? When we come this day, as one great family, to lay our poor offering on the altar, to that God who holds the destinies of nations in his hand, are there none afar off, cast down and sorrowful, who dare not approach the common altar, who cannot put their hands to their hearts, and say, 'Oh, Washington, what art thou to us? Are we not also freemen?' "

As early as 1831 Clay wrote his brother Brutus that if slavery were not eradicated from the republic, there would be a "dissolution of the general government before 50 years—however much it may be deprecated and laughed at now." Again, in the Washington Centennial Address, he dramatized the Webster-Hayne debate in terms of the code duello, foreshadowing the violence of his own future: "The glove is already thrown down . . . the northern and southern champions stand in sullen defiance."

In the years to follow, his intelligence, rhetorical eloquence, and rare force of character were widely acknowledged by both friend and foe. His southern heritage, immense wealth, and northern education seemed to augur a distinguished political career, but his antislavery principles overrode personal ambitions. Many years later, a friend wrote Clay, "The real leaders of nations and races are never allowed to enter their promised lands, and therefore you are always coupled in my mind with regret."

4

FREEDOM HUNTER

CASSIUS RETURNED TO Kentucky in 1832 as master of White Hall. His mother had remarried and was living in Frankfort. All the other children had moved away. Cassius rode over the plantation—or "farm" as even such large estates as his were called in central Kentucky—and checked the crops of tobacco, corn, wheat, hemp, and sugar cane in the bottoms. Brutus, who was farming in Bourbon County, had managed well in his absence and continued to act as his agent. Brutus had seen that the grazing lands were sown with timothy and bluegrass seed during the February snows, thus assuring evenness of growth, and now the cattle and sheep grazed in lush knee-deep pasturage. Cassius visited the distilleries and inspected the ferry. He walked the fencerows and found familiar paths along Jack's Creek, under great forests of poplar, white oak, walnut, elm, wild cherry, hickory, and sycamore trees, leading to a deep bend in the Kentucky River just two miles northwest of the homeplace. He returned by way of the orchard. How he had missed his favorite odors, "which city folks knew so little"! Of all scents in all seasons, those of wild grapevines, crab apples, and fresh hickory nuts were the most delicious.

Now twenty-two years old, Clay had reached his full height; he was well over six feet tall, and agile, strong, big-boned. A portrait of the young Clay by Oliver Frazer looks down today into the circuit courtroom of the Madison County courthouse. One is first aware of the luminosity of the face, as if the young man posing for it had just walked into the light; it is the dark eyes that lend, through contrast, so much light to the clearly molded features. The form is that of a tall man, the height of the shoulders and the fullness of the chest emphasized by a high-collared velvet coat and white shirt. The cravat, or stock, is a mere shadow. The stand-up wings of the shirt collar frame a strong chin and a sensitive, almost feminine mouth. Sable hair, thick as plush, distinctively shaped by a stubborn cowlick on the left side, falls in silky thatches over a high forehead. The left eyebrow, dark as the eyes, is arched like the wing of a hawk and a faint smile curves the lips.

Dr. Warfield had built a new sixteen-room brick mansion, a classic-revival home, north of the Winchester Pike at the east end of Lexington, facing what would later be known as Loudon Avenue. He called it The Meadows, and there in one of its large double parlors Cassius Clay was received with other guests. Mary Jane had developed into a lovely young woman. He and several other suitors were impressed, but their collective admiration was turned into worship by the presence of Mary Jane's elder sister, Anne, who had just returned from an eastern finishing school. A dark-skinned, freckled girl, "with thin hair and person," as Cassius observed, she was "jimber-jawed," so that her nose and chin threatened each other. She had imported "all the follies and habitudes" of the eastern academies; among them was what Cassius Clay termed "the Grecian bend," a vulgar inclination of the body forward "after the manner of some of the classic Venuses." Anne Warfield "seemed at daggers'-points with herself and all the world," Clay said. "As a scandal-monger, she terrorized all Lexington." Of Mary Jane and Anne, he observed, "Never, therefore, had woman so magnificent a foil to set off her charms, as the younger sister had in the elder Warfield."

At social gatherings, Cassius and Mary Jane found themselves often looking at each other. Sometimes she captured the attention of several young men, only to glance lingeringly at Cassius. He was stirred with curiosity. "Was this simplicity," he wondered, "or the highest art?" Not wishing to appear forward, he said no word of love to her—he hardly had the opportunity in such gatherings—yet he knew that she was as much attracted to him as he was to her. One day she told him quietly that she was going "on a certain day hickory-nut-hunting with a few girls," at the home of John Allen, Esquire, in Fayette County. She did not invite him to come. But since Mrs. Allen was his relative, he managed, indeed, to be there when Mary Jane's party arrived.

It was a fine day for hickory-nut-hunting. An October frost had swept the sugar maples, tulip poplars, coffee-beans, gums, and tall hickories, washing them in gold, burning them in crimson fires. The leaves crunched underfoot. The two felt the subdued rays of the October sun through half-nude boughs of trees. Cassius sat on the long grass under the trees and with two small rocks hulled the nuts as others brought them up to the growing pile. Audacious gray squirrels barked at the intruders and scurried about, their long bushy tails plumed over their backs. Mary Jane waited, dawdling, until the others were gone. She was as vivacious as ever, but something was different. Yes, Cassius noted, whereas her dress was often careless, it was today more expensive than usual, and beautifully tailored. Yet her bonnet was thrown back, her hair disordered from exercise. As he looked at her, Mary Jane's eyes sought his. "Come and help me," he said.

She approached him, replying with a tremor in her voice, "I have no seat."

Cassius put his outstretched legs together. "You may sit down here, if you will be mine."

27

Mary Jane hesitated, standing near him now, reddening. Then down she came. Her disordered hair fell over Cassius's face in silky tangles, engulfing him with the aroma of hickory nuts. Murmuring, "I am yours," she withdrew, her cheeks in a transparent glow. Then as their laughing companions approached from the grove, she rose quickly and went off to mingle with them.

The beauty of woman was still a mystery to Cassius Clay. Watching her go, his flushed cheek and sinking heart acknowledged her loveliness. He realized that Mary Jane Warfield had attacked all his senses at once. And he wondered as before, "Was it simplicity, or the highest art?"

Later that day, Mrs. Allen, who had seen Cassius and Mary Jane together, called him aside and said, "Cousin Cash, *don't you marry a Warfield!*" But on that October day his ardor was deaf and his passion blind.

Their wedding was set for February 26, 1833, at The Meadows, but it was not to take place before Cassius had cause to remember Mrs. Allen's warning. Proud old Maria Barr Warfield, nettled at Clay's having requested the hand of her daughter from her husband rather than from her, handed him a letter addressed to Mary Jane. It was from the young lady's disgruntled suitor, John P. Declarey, a physician of Louisville, and contained an attack on Clay's character. Only a few days from his marriage, the young man reflected upon the matter. "It should have been thrown into the fire, and nothing shown to me." Yet as matters stood, the incident had been ballooned into an affair of honor, and "I felt compelled . . . to vindicate myself."

Under this pressure, Clay went to Louisville accompanied by James S. Rollins, the friend he had selected to be his best man. Having procured a small black hickory stick, which he tucked under his arm, Clay confronted his rival on the steps of the Old Inn, Declarey's hotel, and showed him the letter. The physician was ten years

Clay's senior, but of about the same stature. "Do you have any explanations to make, sir?" Clay inquired.

Declarey looked at him and said nothing.

Something about the man, perhaps his hauteur, perhaps his very silence, enraged Clay, and suddenly the two were grappling in the street. With his hickory, Clay began to beat the physician. A crowd gathered. Rollins kept Declarey's friends at bay with a pistol while Clay caned him severely. He left the man on the street, his pride vindicated. "If you desire satisfaction," Clay told him, "I can be found here, at your hotel," and so saying retired with Rollins to his room. In a few hours Clay received a challenge from Declarey, which he promptly accepted.

Twice the men faced each other on the "ground of honor," and both times a large crowd gathered—"Declarey's crowd," Clay said. All parties agreed to defer the meeting. But repeated efforts to arrange the duel fell through. Finally, Declarey's friends proposed that negotiations be held on Clay's wedding day, with the duel to take place that night, February 26, in Louisville. This, Clay noted, "Rollins peremptorily refused." Though a sense of honor might require that he be a few hours late for his wedding, he did not intend to postpone the date for Declarey's convenience. "We had given them a fair chance for a fight," he reasoned. Moreover, he had Rollins publicly announce that they intended to leave by stage for Lexington the next morning. Under the code duello, if Declarey wished to exercise "his usual right of offensive attack in personal rencounter," Clay would be armed and ready to meet him. On the morning of his wedding day, then, Clay and Rollins boarded their stage-coach, "no attack being made."

All day they rode through the cold land to Lexington. "It was quite late in the night," he wrote, "before we reached The Meadows." Mary Jane must have watched for him until her hopes darkened with the day. Then a carriage careened to a stop and she ran to see his tall figure emerge out of the darkness into the light of the entrance hall. Later that night, later than they had expected but still on February 26, the two were married in a candlelit ceremony at The Meadows.

The strange violence of the ill-starred marriage did not end there. During the couple's honeymoon, Clay received messages from friends informing him that Declarey had "denounced me as a coward, and said I was beneath his notice; that he would not pursue me to Lexington, but, if ever he met me in life, he would 'cowhide me.' " At first Clay responded sensibly enough; for a man to leave a newly married wife to return to fight her rejected suitor was "too absurd for even the fool-code." During March the two men exchanged literary barbs in the *Lexington Observer and Reporter.* The "cowhiding" remark—according to the laws of the "fool-code" an insult only blood could wash away—troubled Clay. As angry as he was, though, what goaded him most was the apparent doubt of his courage in the minds of the Warfields.

Clay bided his time, spending short vacations in Cincinnati with the Longworths and with his "wife's connections" in Saint Louis, until, as he stated, "I came to my point of issue, Louisville." There the unsuspecting Declarey got up from his meal and saw Clay leaning against a column in the hotel dining room, his eyes fixed steadily upon the physician. Declarey turned pale and retreated without addressing him. Clay remained a day or more in Louisville, making his presence conspicuous; then seeing that Declarey made no demonstrations, he returned to Lexington. But Clay's calling of the dare apparently disturbed the physician deeply. Having lost Mary Jane, perhaps he could have endured his own despair, but not another bridegroom's happiness. The next evening, Clay wrote, "he committed suicide, by cutting his arteries."

Clay blamed Mrs. Warfield's imprudence—if nothing worse—in causing the death of the unhappy man. She "also sowed the seeds of alienation and distrust in her own household, which in time bore fruit."

By 1835 Clay's life had settled down to one of farming, business, and politics. His first child, Elisha Warfield, was born May 18, and within the next sixteen years Mary Jane would bear eight more of their ten children.*

The political scene in the state was marked by the ever-sharpening conflict between proslavery and antislavery forces that was reflected in shifting allegiances within the Whig party. The American System was under attack from the conservative slaveholding faction. As the newly elected state representative from Madison County, Cassius M. Clay had no wish to endanger his own position or that of other liberal Whigs. He had already perceived that advocacy of abolition stirred violent emotions. Only four years before, the Nat Turner uprising in Virginia—during which the slave-preacher and at least seven other desperate slaves butchered fifty-one men, women, and children in a bloody frenzy—inspired hysterical fear among slaveholders everywhere. In nearby Danville, Kentucky, James G. Birney had outraged the whole central Kentucky region by organizing the Kentucky Anti-Slavery Society, which ignored all proposals for gradual emancipation. During the summer, the Danville community was up in arms because Birney had announced he would publish an abolitionist paper, the *Philanthropist*. Finally the enraged populace so intimidated the printer, S. S. Dismukes, that he sold his shop and slipped out of Danville under cover of darkness.

The upsurge of the bitter slavery issue was to divide the Whig party irrevocably, to destroy many friendships, to

* The children born to the union were Elisha Warfield (1835–1851); Green (1837–1883); Mary Barr (1839–1924); Sarah (Sallie) Lewis (1841–1935); Cassius Marcellus, Jr. (1843–1843, lived three weeks); Cassius Marcellus, Jr. (1845–1857); Brutus Junius (1847–1932); Laura (1849–1941); Flora (1851–1851, lived six weeks); and Anne (Annie) Warfield (1859–1945).

split families, and ultimately, as Clay had predicted at Yale, to place northerner and southerner in a stance of "sullen defiance" against one another. Like Henry Clay, however, Cassius first attempted to mediate between the supporters of Negro slavery and the emancipationists, who desired to bring about its gradual elimination. Speaking to the issue of a constitutional convention to deal with emancipation, the twenty-five-year-old Clay admitted a fear of "dictation and interference rising in the North," at the same time describing slavery as a fatal disease. Moreover, Clay argued that slavery was not only a violation of human rights but also a drain on the potential growth of the commonwealth. From the outset of his career, Clay's support of the American System in Kentucky—industry and free labor, internal improvements, and progressive taxation, for example, over against agrarianism, slave labor, and low taxation—tended to set him apart from his own aristocratic, landowning class.

Putting liberal Whiggery into practice, Clay became a commissioner of the turnpike company that constructed the Lexington-Richmond road. The very names of his business associates in the venture—Squire Turner, Robert Wickliffe, and Waller Bullock—dramatize how rapidly the issue of slavery would split the Whig party: all were soon to become Clay's outspoken enemies.

In 1836 he was beaten in his attempt to return to the legislature because his record was not conservative enough for proslavery interests that increasingly opposed such American System measures as internal improvements. In the courthouse square at Richmond, one old tobacco-raising cynic leaned back in his chair and stated that it was time to "top" young Clay and "let him spread"; but, as Clay observed, "the same cultivators of the plant never liked me any the better after the topping than before."

Returned to Frankfort in 1837, Clay was a solid Whig. He supported improved public schools and the Bank of

Kentucky and looked ahead to a future national bank. During this period he was expanding his own commercial operations beyond White Hall, becoming a nationally known stock breeder and a commissioner of the Northern Bank of Kentucky. He also financed several business ventures, such as partnerships in sawmills and gristmills. But conservatives repeatedly raised obstacles again his programs for commercial expansion.

Within the next few years "Old Duke" Wickliffe, perceiving the threat of the American System to the agricultural slaveowners, publicly denounced Henry Clay, "because I consider him a dangerous politician to the whole of the American States, and especially to the Southern and planting States." Cassius Clay's own active opposition to slavery began as a reaction to the proslavery faction's attack upon the American System and those who favored gradual emancipation. Wickliffe "commenced the agitation of slavery against the Liberals; first through the press, and then against myself and Robert J. Breckinridge upon the stump," Clay wrote.

Never one to back away from a fight, Clay was only too glad to accede to Mary Jane's wishes and move to Lexington—"a more central place," as he put it, for "my headquarters." While retaining White Hall, he purchased one of the most elegant homes in Lexington, the "Lord Morton" house at Limestone and Fifth streets. Having established residence in Fayette County, Clay was a delegate to the national Whig Convention in December 1839, supporting Henry Clay for the presidency. The other Kentucky delegates were in agreement, but in spite of all Clay could do as floor leader, Harrison and Tyler carried the day.

It was at the 1839 convention that Cassius Clay first met Horace Greeley. He was never to forget the man's "large head, thinly covered with auburn hair, approaching white, and his boyish, innocent-looking, and amiable face," which to him indicated "genius and great simplicity of character." Greeley also was impressed, and he opened the columns of the *New York Tribune* to Clay's letters, ultimately giving his views national visibility.

Clay returned to the Bluegrass and continued his fight at home against the proslavery interests. In the election of 1840, he successfully opposed Robert Wickliffe, Jr., son of the "Old Duke," and in so doing earned the burning hatred of slaveholding politicians. Specifically, Clay opposed the repeal of a statute of 1833, known as the "Negro Law," which prohibited the importation of slaves into Kentucky for sale. Taking his lead from proslavery representatives in the House in Washington, however, "Old Duke" Wickliffe tried to invoke a gag rule. He equated Clay's discussion of the issue with the danger of insurrection and ultimately accused him of being an abolitionist.

Clay's answer was defiant. He denounced slavery as an evil—"morally, economically, physically, intellectually, socially, religiously, politically—evil in its inception, in its duration, and in its catastrophe." Yet, he was sagacious enough to declare himself a gradual emancipationist. Joined by such men as Robert J. Breckinridge and Thomas F. Marshall, Clay withstood the attack of the Wickliffes and their supporters upon the "Negro Law" and kept it from being repealed until 1849. During this same crucial 1840 session of the legislature, Clay also voted to establish the Kentucky Institution for the Education of the Blind.

By 1841 he was drawn into open warfare with the slave power. "They knew their strength," Clay observed, "and . . . determined to crush all liberal thought . . . in the bud." Breckinridge, Marshall, and others who had sided with Clay withdrew from the fray as the violence increased, but "Cash" Clay boldly denounced slavery. Against the advice of Henry Clay, who had foreseen the savagery, Clay entered the 1841 campaign, which was to end on a note of tension and violence that would not be relieved for years. The campaign was marked by inflammatory speeches, noisy partisans, and torchlight processions. Clay's opponent was again Robert Wickliffe, Jr., and as tensions mounted, Wickliffe introduced Mary Jane Clay's name in a speech, contending that she and all the Warfields "were opposed to Clay and were secretly fighting him." "I took exception," said Clay of his response to Wickliffe's charge, disdaining it "as inadmissible." The result was a duel between the contestants.

Clay later wrote in explanation of his decision to fight: "I wanted to show those who lived by force, that it would be met, at all times, and in all places, with force." At Locust Grove, just outside Louisville, the antagonists faced each other at ten paces, raised and fired their pistols. Both missed. Clay then held his pistol above his head and demanded another fire, but the good sense of the seconds prevailed and the matter was dropped.

Again in 1843, Clay was lured into a nearly fatal fight with Samuel M. Brown, a paid assassin from New Orleans who was said to be undefeated in forty fights. By this time Clay was openly advocating emancipation and specifically attacking the proslavery element of the Whig party. During the Wickliffe-Garrett Davis debate at Russell's Cave Spring, Clay stood and began to take issue with the Wickliffe faction of the party. Brown struck him with a club and gave him the "damned lie."

Clay was aware of the man's reputation and knew that a death struggle was imminent. He drew his bowie knife and was starting toward his assailant when he was seized from behind and borne fifteen feet away from Brown.

Brown raised his Colt revolver and cried, "Clear the way, and let me kill the damned rascal!"

The two men confronted each other in sudden isolation. Clay had either to run or advance. Turning his left side and covering it with his arm, he moved toward Brown rapidly with his weapon in his right fist. Brown took deliberate aim and, when Clay was upon him, fired at his heart. But Clay came down upon his head with a tremendous blow that opened a three-inch slit in Brown's skull through to the brain. The mob struck Clay with hickory sticks and chairs, but he used his weapon with astonishing celerity. He freed his arms from the grappling mob and his knife slashed ferociously in circles. Brown's nose suddenly became two, separated with an oozing red cleft; an eye was gouged from its socket; one ear dangled at his cheek. Another vermilion groove opened across his skull—another—another. Finally, in order to save Brown, the conspirators thwarted Clay long enough to throw the hired killer over a stone fence, where he fell down a steep descent into the waters of Russell's Cave Spring.

One letter of an eyewitness, complete with misspellings, provides an added insight into Clay's extraordinary skill with the bowie knife:

> You have heard of the . . . fight at the Cave. It was not slow. It was the first Bowie knife fight I ever saw, and the way . . . *Cash* used it was tremendious. Blows on the head hard enough to cleave a man's skull asunder, but Brown must have a skull of extraordinary thickness. He stood the blows as well if not better than most of men would do. Cassius most gallantly faced and even advanced on his six barrel revolving pistol, which alone saved his life. He sprang in upon him and used the knife with such power that Brown was either paralyzed by the blows, or forgot his revolver.

Having felt the impact of the bullet upon his breast, Clay believed himself mortally wounded. He raised his bloody knife and declared, "I stand ready to defend the truth." No one, neither the Wickliffes nor any of their followers, was in any mood to take up the challenge.

Clay's friends took him to a nearby house and opened his vest and shirt, revealing the scabbard strapped to his chest. Near the silver-lined point was the indentation of the bullet. Fingers raised the sheath gingerly, and the flattened lead bullet fell out. To the amazement of all, the only wound was a red spot over Clay's heart.

Clay never gloried in his reputation as a fighting man. "On the contrary," he wrote, "it has always been a source of annoyance to me; overshadowing that to which I most aspired—a high and self-sacrificing moral courage—where the mortal was to be sacrificed to the immortal." Of the Russell's Cave Spring episode, he observed, "Providence, or fate, reserved for me a better work." Reflecting upon which power was responsible for "my many escapes from death"—the God of his mother or the Deity of his father, operating through "moral and physical laws"—Clay averred, "Certain it is that he who stands on the right may often hold his own against hosts in arms."

5

FIREBRAND!

IN THE NEXT term of court, Clay found himself arraigned
before the circuit judge on a charge of mayhem. The trial
took place in the old Fayette County courthouse with its
spire-topped cupola and four-faced clock. By all accounts,
the fiery politician faced a proslavery jury. Volunteering
to defend him were his talented brother-in-law, John
Speed Smith, and Henry Clay. Although the weight of
evidence was with the defense, the makeup of the jury
and proslavery attitudes of the community left the outcome in considerable doubt.

The packed courtroom was charged with suspense as
Henry Clay rose, a tall, commanding figure, graceful in
manner and movement. Standing as near the jury as
possible, he spoke to them in reassuring, familiar tones of
a common Kentucky heritage, of their common pride in a
common soil, of the great honor they had done him in the
past in permitting him to serve them, and of the majesty of
the law of the commonwealth they all loved and impar-
tially respected—no matter what their differences on
issues. If they would bear with him, he wished to say to
them what he believed, in their hearts, they already
knew:

The question which this jury of freemen is called upon their
honor and conscience to decide, is not whether the political

views and sentiments of the prisoner were just or not, nor whether they agreed or disagreed with yours; nor yet, if they were just, whether ill-timed or out of place. You are bound, on your oaths, to say, was Clay acting in his constitutional and legal right? Was he aggressive, or resting peaceably in the security of the laws which guard alike the safety of you, and me, and him? And yet more: Did he occupy even higher ground than all human enactments—the eternal laws of self-defense—which come only of God, and which none but He can annul, judge, or punish: Standing, as he did, without aiders or abettors, and without popular sympathy; with the fatal pistol of conspired murderers pointed at his heart, would you have had him meanly and cowardly fly? Or would you have him to do just what he did do—there stand in defense, or there fall?

Suddenly Henry Clay turned toward Cassius, saying, "And, if he had not, he would not have been *worthy of the name which he bears!"* Within the hour the jury found the defendant not guilty.

The outcome of the trial indicated that Clay could attract the respect of those who disagreed with his principles. Striking in appearance, courageous, intelligent, colorful, he could, if he had been willing to support the more conservative faction of the Whig party, have attained high political office. Certainly he had nothing to gain personally from espousing the antislavery movement in Kentucky. Indeed, he had much to lose—friends, fortune, even his life.

In 1844 the Whig party nominated Henry Clay to carry the presidential banner against the relatively unknown James K. Polk of Tennessee, who represented the Democrats and the foremost of proslavery issues, the annexation of Texas. Both the Clays were opposed to the admission of Texas to the Union as a slave state, although Cassius was the more outspoken in his charges. To him the Texas question was simply a scheme to extend slavery and to gain congressional leverage for slaveholding interests.

When it became evident that the abolitionists in the East were likely to cut into the Whig vote for Henry Clay by running their own candidate, James G. Birney, in their "hopeless cause," Henry Clay asked "Cousin Cash" to campaign in that region for him. By this time, Cassius Clay had freed his unentailed slaves at White Hall, and his presence in the North during a grueling three-month campaign made a powerful impression. Everywhere he was received with enthusiasm, and on Boston Common, after Daniel Webster had spoken, the cry for "Clay" was "like the near ocean's roar." Still he was not radical enough to suit the northern abolitionists. They contended that they had the constitutional right "to abolish the slave trade between the several states, and having the power," were "bound to carry [it] into sudden execution." Herein, Clay believed, "they diverge from the mass of their fellow-citizens of the free states, and begin for the first time to become dangerous to the slave states." Contradicting such abolitionist views, Clay declared, "I stand opposed to the power of congress to interfere with the slaves at all." In his judgment, abolitionists committed the grave error of attacking the Constitution; their efforts brought disruption to the Union rather than a rational solution to the problem of slavery. They saw their duties as citizens of the republic too narrowly. They should rather, he contended, stand for "the Union and the Constitution at the same time."

Challenged by the ultra Liberty party men of the North, who demanded to know how he could support a slave-holder for president, Clay replied, "I wish [Henry Clay] were not. Yet it does not become *me*, who have so lately ceased to be a slaveholder myself, to condemn him." He pursued the Texas issue vigorously, and proclaimed the slogan, *"Clay, Union, and Liberty!"* over against *"Polk, Slavery, and Texas."*

But Henry Clay had a wide fence to straddle between the slaveholding Whigs of the South and the antislavery Whigs of the North. On September 18, 1844, he wrote

Cassius Clay a confidential letter from Ashland of his troubles. "At the North, I am represented as an ultra supporter of the institution of slavery, whilst at the South I am described as an Abolitionist; when I am neither the one nor the other." Southern Whigs, Henry Clay believed, were turning Cassius Clay's antislavery views against his candidacy; "hence," he wrote, "the necessity of the greatest circumspection, and especially that you should avoid committing me." Henry Clay sent the letter to Willis Green, to be passed on to Cassius Clay through Horace Greeley, but it never got to Clay and was published in the *New York Democrat*. The effect was to reduce Clay's authority as a spokesman for the Whig leader's moderate emancipationist views. Wavering Liberty party members interpreted the letter, so Clay reported, as "proof of his infidelity to principle." The upshot was that they turned to Birney. By siphoning off more than 60,000 votes, the Birney abolitionists allowed Polk, a proslavery southern Democrat, to claim New York by a plurality of 5,106 votes. Cassius Clay himself was first aware of the results as he rode southward on his stage toward Maysville. At the bottom of a mountain, suspended from a newly erected hickory pole, the leaves still green on top, was a skinned coon. "Then we knew," he remarked, "the Whigs, nicknamed 'Coons,' were lost!"

Clay blamed the abolitionist extremists for the defeat of Henry Clay, in his judgment "the most honest man, next to Lincoln, that ever ran for President." But he also held the Whigs culpable for dividing themselves on petty matters "while the South subjected all its differences to the major issue of perpetuating the unqualified evil of slavery."

Yet Clay believed that his campaigning in the free states had not been a total loss, for he perceived an awakening in the souls of men. "However illogical in a political sense," Clay wrote, "this nucleus of moral protest against slavery . . . aroused the better sentiments of the nation." Moreover, "the slave power was put upon its necessity of disproving that slavery was the 'sum of all villainies.' " He was later to write: "These were the aggressive forces which ultimately drew all others into their train; till the Free-Soil Party, and next the Republican Party, stood on one side, and the Pro-Slavery Party on the other, under the banner of False Democracy. And thus was brought on the Civil War, and the overthrow of Slavery."

After the election the defeated candidate was honored at a dinner in Lexington at Dr. Benjamin W. Dudley's home. Cassius Clay was in attendance, along with Senator James T. Morehead, former governor of Kentucky. Frustrated at his defeat by so inferior an opponent as James K. Polk, Henry Clay was in no mood for good fellowship. Cassius Clay observed that "Mr. Clay took his defeat with ill grace, and showed more than his usual impatience." In a few words, he displayed "that unhappy arrogance which was fatal to his political personal success." First he took Morehead to task for some minor difference, "in the style of a superior lecturing a delinquent." Unappeased by Morehead's apology, the elder statesman then turned his wrath upon the abolitionists of New York, glancing at his cousin as he severely denounced them. Cassius Clay himself had already been badgered by the press and denounced by his local enemies for his speeches in the North. Now indignant at the lecturing of "poor Morehead," he was in no humor "to submit quietly even to the petulance of Henry Clay." Moreover, he noted, "I could but feel that part of his censure was against myself."

So when the ire of the great man at last subsided and he sat down, Cassius Clay stood up and answered him. "Mr. Clay, whatever errors of judgment, or of patriotism, may justly be imputed to the Abolitionists, I think you are the last man who ought to complain; for, if I remember aright, you said that the Abolitionists should be set apart from, and denounced by all parties; so they but played the *rôle* you marked out for them."

White Hall in 1894

Photograph by Isaac Jenks
Courtesy of
J. Winston Coleman, Jr.

Clay as a young man

Portrait by Oliver Frazer in Madison County courthouse

Mary Jane Warfield

Portrait by G. P. A. Healey   *Courtesy of Miss Esther Bennett*

Middle-aged Clay

Matthew Brady Imperial Mezzotint   *Courtesy of Miss Esther Bennett*

Clay in uniform of Major General, about 1863

Courtesy of Lincoln Memorial University

Green Clay (eldest son of Cassius Clay)

Courtesy of Mrs. William H. Townsend and Mrs. Joe H. Murphy

Brutus J. Clay (second son of Cassius Clay)

Courtesy of Mr. and Mrs. Floyd G. Clay

Sarah (Sallie) Clay

Courtesy of Mrs. William H. Townsend and Mrs. Joe H. Murphy

Laura Clay

Mary Barr Clay

Courtesy of Mrs. William H. Townsend
and Mrs. Joe H. Murphy

Anne Clay

Courtesy of Mrs. William H. Townsend and Mrs. Joe H. Murphy

Launey (Leonide Petroff) Clay, about 1878

Courtesy of Mrs. William H. Townsend and Mrs. Joe H. Murphy

Marie Petipa, March 22, 1865

Courtesy of Mrs. William H. Townsend and Mrs. Joe H. Murphy

Marie Petipa, May 1, 1865

Courtesy of Mrs. William H. Townsend and Mrs. Joe H. Murphy

Portrait of unnamed ballerina

Courtesy of White Hall State Shrine

Dora Richardson Clay

Courtesy of Mrs. William H. Townsend and Mrs. Joe H. Murphy

Clay on his second wedding day

Photograph by Isaac Jenks   *Courtesy of J. Winston Coleman, Jr.*

Henry Clay's admirers and followers looked on in shocked astonishment. The Sage of Ashland said nothing. The two were ever afterward cool toward each other. In Cassius Clay's view, the Whigs were "sore unto death," and as usual "someone must be made the scapegoat. I was the most agreeable sacrifice to them, for obvious reasons." Clay did not take the role of scapegoat lightly. "If it had not been for me," he said, "there would have been none of the slavery muddle, and they might have been eating treasury cheese, like other old rats, without hinderance."

On January 18, 1845, Cassius Clay, in his "Address to the People of Kentucky," emphasized once again the economic, moral, and cultural disadvantages of slavery. The impressions of his trip through the East and the petty spite and vengefulness of the proslavery Whigs upon his return combined to confirm the rightness of his course. "I needed no urging on," he said, "for I had seen a vitality in the popular heart in my Northern tour which foreshowed the downfall of the slave-power." Whereas slavery a few years before was looked upon as a matter of course, "Now," he stated, "few are so hardy as to deny that some twenty or thirty years will witness its extinction. The time is, in my judgment, yet nearer at hand." Clay foresaw a coalition of antislavery Whigs and members of the growing Liberty party of the East. He was convinced this coalition would eventually defeat the proslavery Whigs and Democrats of both North and South.

The *Lexington Observer and Reporter* had denounced Clay's opinions as "militant and provocative" and closed its columns to him, but he did not despair of a forum for his emancipationist views. On February 19, 1845, he announced his prospectus for publication of the *True American*, "a paper devoted to gradual and constitutional emancipation." He specified, "The press under our control will appeal *temperately* but *firmly* to the interests and the reason, and not to the passions, of our people; we shall take care rigidly to respect the legal rights of others, because we intend to *maintain our own*."

Clay was well aware of the risks of his undertaking. Twice mobs in Danville had attacked James G. Birney's antislavery paper, the *Philanthropist*, and the abolitionist had fled to Cincinnati. Lexington was a far more broadminded city than Danville, it was true, but the conservative editor of the *Observer and Reporter* harangued Clay in the same issue in which his prospectus appeared: "Mr. Clay has taken the very worst time that he could to begin the agitation of this great and delicate question . . . since the fanatical crusade which has been waged by Northern Abolitionists against . . . slavery . . . has produced a state of feeling in the minds of slaveholders anything but propitious to the slave or his liberation."

In questioning Clay's project, the editor was, of course, alerting slaveholders themselves: "We make these remarks not to discourage Mr. Clay, for we know very well that his ardent and enthusiastic temperament never sees an obstacle in his way . . . but to apprise him in advance, that . . . he is embarked in a very hopeless undertaking."

Giving in neither to condescension nor to fear, Clay went on with determination. His prospectus was, in his own words, "moderate enough—proposing none but constitutional methods in the overthrow of slavery." But by the time of his first issue, which appeared June 3, 1845, under the motto GOD AND LIBERTY!, as Clay later wrote, "the war was raging apace, all along the lines." Doubtless he was referring both to the editors of the *Observer and Reporter* and to Robert Wickliffe of the *Kentucky Gazette* when he charged his opponents with taking the ground that "the subject of slavery shall not be discussed, and . . . violence shall suppress our press." In answer Cassius quoted the Constitution: "Congress shall make no law . . . abridging the freedom of speech or the press." But he saved his bitterest invective for his archenemy, "Old Duke" Wickliffe: "Old man, remember . . . Russell's cave; and if you still thirst for bloodshed and violence, the same blade that repelled the assaults of assassin[s'] sons, once more in self-defence, is ready to drink of the blood of the hireling horde of sycophants and outlaws of the assassin-sire of assassins."

Clay had also prepared carefully to fend off "*mobleaders*," whom he anathematized as "inevitable cowards," while at the same time frankly admitting that he was "not so Quixotic as to seek to fight with a mob; we know that we can be overpowered by numbers; yet, from the defence of our own known rights, we are not to be deterred by vague threats of real dangers, coming from any man or set of men."

The story has long since passed into legend in the Bluegrass—how Clay procured the three-story red brick building in Lexington at Number 6, North Mill Street, and with six or eight loyal friends prepared the office of the *True American* for the siege. Among his associates were William L. Neal; William and Black Kinkaid, both prominent citizens; and Clay's faithful friend, immigrant engineer Major Thomas Lewinski, who later was the architect in charge of remodeling White Hall.

Clay and his friends lined the outside doors and window shutters of the building with sheet iron to prevent burning. He purchased two small brass cannons at Cincinnati, loaded them to the muzzle with bullets, slugs, and nails, and placed them breast-high on a table at the entrance, directly across from double doors opening in the middle and fastened with a chain "so that only one person at a time could make his way in to certain death." Mexican lances and an ample number of muskets lined the walls of the printing office. In the event these measures should fail to stop a lawless entry, he arranged an escape by trapdoors leading to the roof and across buildings. He reserved a keg of powder with which to blow the establishment and everybody in it into atoms when resistance became no longer possible. "This," he stated, "I should most certainly have done, in case of the last extremity," for "I knew that if the office was once taken, after the bloody defense I intended to make, my life was forfeited, and I was determined to fire my magazine and send as many of them into eternity in my company as possible."

The paper had scarcely been launched when Clay published this letter:

C. M. Clay:

You are meaner than the autocrats of hell. You may think you can awe and curse the people of Kentucky to your infamous course. You will find, when it is too late for life, the people are no cowards. Eternal hatred is locked up in the bosoms of braver men, your betters, for you. The hemp is ready for your neck. Your life cannot be spared. Plenty thirst for your blood—are determined to have it. It is unknown to you and your friends, if you have any, and in a way you little dream of.

Revengers.

A more temperate editor might have torn up the threat and tried to forget it, but Clay used it as a demonstration of the desperate iniquity of the slave power. "The truth is," he observed, "the mob was worse scared than I."

After the first issue, Horace Greeley hailed the *True American* in the *New York Tribune* as "the first paper which ever bearded the monster in his den, and dared him to a most unequal encounter." Slavery was the burning issue of the day, and interest in the paper was so intense that by August 12 the subscription list had more than doubled—reaching about 700 subscribers in Kentucky and about 2,700 in other states.

The editor exhorted the 600,000 citizens of Kentucky to cease the subordination of "their true prosperity to the real, or supposed interests of some [31,000] slaveholders, thus submitting themselves as willing slaves to a despotic and irresponsible minority." The price of slavery, he insisted, was the lack of industry. This impoverished the small farmer and factory worker alike. He illustrated his arguments with pungent facts. "In Louisville you pay about ten cents a head for killing hogs; in Cincinnati, the killer pays, on the contrary, the seller ten cents a head for the privilege of killing. Why the difference? In Cincinnati the hair is made into mattresses, the bristles into brushes, the blood into some chemical preparations, the hoofs into glue, the fat into lard and oil." Clay's pocketbook arguments began to win over farmers and laborers who, in many cases, were not even subscribers to his paper but heard the courthouse talk.

Clay invited and published various points of view on the slavery question, but he also ranged widely into subjects of topical interest. In the June 17 paper, he editorialized upon the death of Andrew Jackson ("Like Sylla he never spared an enemy or forgot a friend."). In the same issue, under the caption "Give the Devil His Due," he good-humoredly recognized "Old Duke" Wickliffe's decency in saving an innocent Negro from lynching. Again, in the same issue, he linked the frequency of divorce in the South with slavery, and urged the southern women, "Put away your slaves. . . . If you want to drink, go to the pump or to the spring and get it; if to bathe, prepare your own bath, or plunge into the running stream; make your own beds, sweep your own rooms, and wash your own clothes; throw away corsets and nature herself will form your bustles. Then you will have full chests, glossy hair, rosy complexions, smooth velvet skins, muscular, rounded limbs, graceful tournures, elasticity of person, eyes of alternate fire and most melting languor; generous hearts, sweet tempers, good husbands, long lives of honeymoons, and—*no divorces.*"

The *Christian Intelligencer* of Georgetown supported Clay's political views, thus bringing thousands of Methodists closer to the emancipationist fold. A paper similar to Clay's was in the planning stages in Louisville, and even the proslavery Democratic press of the Green River section of Kentucky, west of Lexington, had reprinted one of the *True American* articles and, in Clay's view, "seemed ready to wage a common war" against "the ruinous competition of slave labor with that of whites." Indeed, now for the first time it appeared to Clay that men of good will and emancipation interests, crossing party affiliations, were about to come together into an effective force "for the overthrow of slavery in a legal way."

While Clay's illusion of victory was forming, danger was closing in. Exhausted with the struggle to launch his paper, to carry on an enormous correspondence, to provide for the defense of the *True American*, and to plan for a "friends of emancipation" convention to be held the next Fourth of July in Frankfort, Clay contracted typhoid fever about the middle of July. Heavy pressures bore down upon the stricken editor. Lexington was the very citadel of slavery in Kentucky, and its most powerful proslavery organ, the *Observer and Reporter*, had accurately read the danger signs in Clay's success. By July 16, the slavery interests it represented were in no mood for further toleration and demanded "*peace*" from "the *agitation* of a most delicate subject." In response to Clay's proposed convention for emancipationists, the *Observer* asked: "Slaveholders of Fayette, is it not now time for you to act on this matter yourself, and as conventions are all the fashion at this time, hold one yourself?" In reviling Horace Greeley and the *New York Tribune*, "deeply tinctured with abolition tendencies," the editor made his application to Clay's *True American*, and to Clay himself, clear enough. There were no conventions of slaveholders, of course, but within the next few weeks they met in secret conclaves, while their supporters began to gather in the streets and around the Fayette County courthouse.

Abraham Lincoln's father-in-law, Robert Todd, was the Whig party's candidate for the state legislature. During the month before the three-day election of August 4–6, his campaign against the militant proslavery Independent,

Colonel Charles C. Moore, reached a heated pitch. Moore favored repeal of the 1833 statute forbidding the further importation of slaves to Kentucky—the "iniquitous Negro Law," as conservative slaveholders called it. Although a slaveholder himself, Todd, like Cassius Clay before him, refused to support repeal of the Non-Importation Act on grounds of sound policy. The balloting was extremely close. Only a dramatic last-moment appearance of Henry Clay, touring the polling places with candidate Todd in an open carriage, saved the election for the rallying Whigs. But it was a costly gesture for the Old Chieftain, for in revenge, an incendiary set fire to his bagging factory and it burned to the ground. The story of the conflagration was carried in the *Observer* on August 9, 1845. Many of the most fanatical of Colonel Moore's supporters, including "nigger traders" and such leaders as Wickliffe, who wished to expand their traffic and breeding of slaves, placed the blame for their stinging defeat at the steel-sheeted doors of Cash Clay and his "firebrand" *True American*.

While the excitement rose, Clay languished with typhoid fever in his house on Limestone Street. During late July and early August friends edited the paper for him, while he dictated his work from a sickbed. One of the leading articles, a guest opinion diverging from his own, advocated an ideal environment for slaves—education, religion, and "usefulness and citizenship"—while warning southern slaveholders that they were surrounded by free people on all sides. "Everything trenches on [the slaveholder's] infected district," so the article ran, "and the wolf looks calmly in upon his fold." Clay, meanwhile, pulled his fevered thoughts together and dictated an editorial which, together with the article in the same issue of Tuesday, August 12, struck flames of fury into the tinderbox that was Lexington: "But remember, you who dwell in marble palaces, that there are strong arms and fiery hearts and iron pikes in the streets, and panes of glass only between them and the silver plate on the board, and the smooth skinned woman on the ottoman. When you have mocked at virtue, denied the agency of God in the affairs of men, and made rapine your honeyed faith, tremble! for the day of retribution is at hand, and the masses will be avenged."

After Clay had published his inflammatory editorial, a ride to the *True American* office caused a relapse. On Thursday, August 14, he was informed that a meeting of citizens was being held in the courthouse. He dragged himself from bed, dressed, and armed himself. Against the remonstrances of Mary Jane and his family, he made his way into the assemblage—a group of about thirty men who were ready to suppress his "abolition" paper. These leaders of the Lexington community, especially Clay's enemy Thomas F. Marshall, whom he had recently attacked editorially as the "apostate Whig" and helped to defeat in an election, were denouncing him. He later wrote that they had "utterly misconceived" and "tortured from its true meaning" both the article and the editorial in the *True American* of August 12. Whig D. M. Craig entered "in a most lachrymose mood," and while first avowing himself "my personal friend," then expressed "his determination to use his musket against my life." Clay lay on a bench, raising himself from time to time to answer. When he finally demanded a hearing, he was clamorously denied it and informed that he was in a "*private* meeting." Faint and with parched lips, Clay arose and, proclaiming that he was "far from intruding myself upon any set of men," staggered out the door and made his way once more to his bed, exhausted by the effort.

Later the same day, Thomas H. Waters entered Clay's chamber to deliver a letter in the name of a three-man committee representing "a number of the respectable citizens of the city." It stated their collective desire that Clay discontinue publication of the *True American* and further declared:

Your paper is agitating and exciting our community to an extent of which you can scarcely be aware. We do not approach you in the form of a threat. But we owe it to you to state, that, in our judgment, your own safety, as well as the repose and peace of the community, are involved in your answer. We await your reply. . . . We are instructed to report your answer to a meeting, tomorrow evening [i.e., on Friday, Aug. 15] at three o'clock, and will expect it by two o'clock, P.M., of tomorrow.

The committee members did not have to wait long for a reply. Clay belittled their power and defied their action. "Your advice with regard to my personal safety," he concluded, "is worthy of the source whence it emanated, and meets with the same contempt from me which the purposes of your mission excite. Go tell your secret conclave of cowardly assassins that C. M. Clay knows his rights and how to defend them." The next day the reply was printed, preceded by the committee's letter, in an extra edition of the *True American*. Several handbills followed through the weekend, in which Clay attempted to explain his constitutional position to the populace. As he dictated, his hands and head were continually bathed with cold water to keep his fever down to a point below delirium.

Meanwhile, after the three-man committee had left his home Thursday evening, Clay again dragged himself to Number 6, North Mill Street. There, he said, "I immediately made preparations for the defence of my office." He saw that the powder in the cannons was fresh and dry, the bullets, slugs, and nails tightly packed. The menacing snouts of both weapons were trained, breast-high, upon the double entrance doors with the secured chain. The lances were honed to razor sharpness. Muskets, shotguns, and pistols were primed and loaded. Clay's bowie knife hung in its sheath over his sweating chest. He warned his chosen friends to be ready, "to which they manfully assented." He then wrote his will. No attack was made that night. The next morning, Friday, August 15, Clay sent for his camp bed because "I was unable to sit up."

More than 500 "unanimous" men had gathered at the courthouse by three o'clock; but then, in Clay's view, they did not "come up to their threats." They had demanded that he agree to shut down his press, or forfeit his personal safety. But when they found "I was still able to drag my feeble body to the place of attack, and rally around me many brave hearts," Clay charged, "they basely cowered: gave up all hope of a successful attack, and put off the contest for three days, well-knowing that before then, from the report of my physicians, I would be dead, or unable to lead my friends." Indeed, the leaders of the mob found it necessary to seek more public support. They sent runners with handbills to adjoining counties to call in all proslavery enthusiasts, rallying them to "the suppression of *The True American*." Many bills bore the slogan "to hell with Clay."

Learning these facts, the exhausted editor was satisfied that he had done all his conscience demanded and all the Constitution supported in responding to the iniquitous threat. Under extraordinary pressures, he had defended both his life and his press. He had made his point. Seeing that no mob, at least for the time being, would force him from the building, reeling on the verge of collapse, he finally responded to the inner voice of wisdom, faintly echoing his democratic faith in the people and the laws. "I told my friends to disarm the office, and leave it to the untrammeled decision of the citizens."

Clay then went home and dictated his program for emancipation, working an hour past midnight so that it could be published the next day, August 16. He favored a constitutional convention and stated, "I would say that every female slave, born after a certain day and year, should be free at the age of twenty-one," for in time this "would gradually, and at last, make our state truly free." For slaveholders who insisted upon "equity" and "rights," he simply reminded them that "the blacks also have rights . . . and surely . . . the slaveholder has the lion's share." He found the idea of the amalgamation of the races "absurd," and concerning blacks' engaging in politics, he advised, "let after generations act for themselves."

Exhausted and as ill as ever, Clay despaired of being able to be present at the meeting on Monday, August 18. Bathed continuously in cold water, he struggled against delirium. "Every relative believed," he later wrote, "I would be murdered on Monday, and all, but my wife and mother, advised me to yield up the liberty of the press: but I preferred rather to die."

The 1,200 people who gathered in the courthouse yard at eleven o'clock on Monday, harangued by the eloquent Thomas F. Marshall to a fever pitch of outrage, were not to be calmed with reason or compromise. "They wanted me to say that I would cease the discussion . . . of slavery," Clay said, "for well did they see, from a brief experience, that slavery and a free press could not live together."

On the same Monday morning, the city judge, George R. Trotter, issued an injunction against the *True American* office "and all its appurtenances." The city marshal called on Clay. Only then, when served with the legal writ, did Clay yield up the keys. He turned over on his sickbed and wept bitter tears.

At the mass meeting, a group called the Committee of Sixty was appointed, with James B. Clay, the son of Henry Clay, acting as its secretary. According to a resolution offered by Marshall and approved by the assembly, they were "to repair to the office of the *True American*, take possession of the press and printing apparatus, pack up the same, and place it at the railroad office for transportation."

When they reached the Mill Street office, however, Mayor James Logue was waiting. He warned them that they were committing an illegal act, which he was bound to resist. But Logue was outnumbered. He surrendered the keys and possession of the building. The committee members carried out their charge and returned to the courthouse at about three o'clock in the afternoon, when the meeting was adjourned.

Up at the corner of Fifth and Limestone, Clay raved in delirium.

There were many Lexingtonians who called the deed "dignified." The *Observer* commended the "innumerable body of citizens" for accomplishing their purpose "without the slightest damage to property or the effusion of a drop of blood."

Clay, of course, dissented. By September 25 he was well enough to pen his "appeal to Kentucky and to the world," declaring, "Thus, on the 18th day of August, 1845, were the Constitutional liberties of Kentucky overthrown; and an irresponsible despotism of slaveholding established in their ruins."

Clay's health was gradually restored, and by October the *True American* was in business again, printed in Cincinnati but datelined Lexington, where Clay continued to reside and edit the paper. In Horace Greeley's phrase, Clay conducted it "with no abatement in the vigor or plainness of his reprobation of Human Bondage." The paper continued under his direct editorship up to June 7, 1846, when he left it in the hands of John C. Vaughan to volunteer for the Mexican War. In December 1847 the *True American* was succeeded by the *Louisville Examiner.*

Locally, Clay was considered a "firebrand," one who had broken from his aristocratic caste and defied all conventions. But his name was on the tongues of people throughout the North and East—and of people everywhere who had no sympathy for the oligarchy of slaveholders. In the winter that followed, thousands heard him speak.

But tens of thousands who had never seen him remembered August 18 as a day of martyrdom. Years later, in his

Political Recollections, A. W. Blinn spoke for such people, recalling "the shame and sorrow that filled millions of hearts on hearing that a mob had destroyed that free press."

Clay's name, Blinn wrote, "was thence a synonym for heroism."

6

PRELUDE TO TRAGEDY

Since early March 1846, news had been coming to the Bluegrass of the advance of General Zachary Taylor's troops over the 150 miles of disputed sandy plains between Corpus Christi, on the Nueces River, and the Rio Grande to the south. As a southern Democrat, President Polk was committed to "all of Texas," but the real prize lay in California, with its green valleys and the harbor of San Francisco. Rumors that it might be pounced upon by the British, already near at hand and irritated over the Oregon issue, added to Polk's eagerness to take California—if necessary by war with weaker Mexico. While Whigs contended with Democrats over the boundaries, proud Mexico declared Texas in rebellion. In late April, Captain S. B. Thornton and his scouting party were ambushed by Mexican troops north of the Rio Grande. Polk now had his chance for war: blood had been spilled on "Texas soil," and one brave officer taken prisoner.

Since 1843 Clay had opposed the annexation of Texas in numerous speeches and articles, predicting that slavery interests would eventually push the country into an unjustified war with Mexico. May 16, 1846, he reported on a "War Meeting" for the pages of the *True American*. Curious citizens packed the Fayette County courthouse and its galleries. Whig speakers condemned the imminent hostilities and called the Mexican affair "Polk's War," while proslavery Democrats spoke of "manifest destiny."

The audience quieted as General Leslie Combs of the Kentucky Militia entered and ascended the dais, where a map hung on the wall. Clay sardonically observed that the disputed area was "called Texas" and "put in *blue!*" Rattan in hand, Combs proceeded to brief the audience. Taylor had already occupied his important munitions and supply source, Point Isabel on the Gulf of Mexico, at the mouth of the Rio Grande. But now he had moved inland, up the valley of the Rio Grande about twenty or thirty miles, and established a new position at Fort Brown, directly across the Rio Grande from the Mexican city of Matamoros. According to Combs's analysis, Taylor's 2,200 troops were spread dangerously thin and "liable to attack in divers places."

Clay's article satirized Combs as having commanded only "*corn-stalk* militia!" and ragged him for belaboring the obvious. And it lashed out at the president: "We solemnly protest against the damning usurpation of James K. Polk in *making* war without the consent of Congress."

Four days later, Lexington was full of bustle and excitement. Cheapside, the traditional public gathering place, erupted with talk of "Old Zack" Taylor and strange, faraway places, as people waited for "the speaking." Horses and carriages were thick beneath the spreading maple trees in front of the Phoenix Hotel on Main Street. Blue and gold of militia uniforms dominated the colorful tide of humanity, and blood surged into animated faces as "our boys" and "the Stars and Stripes" punctuated conversations about the two recent victories of Taylor's troops at Palo Alto and Resaca de la Palma. Yes, they all agreed, it appeared that President Polk had his war with Mexico after all; the firebrand, Cash Clay, was right about that. On May 11, Polk had sent a war message to

Congress, and the United States was, indeed, formally at war with Mexico. Now the call had gone out for 50,000 volunteers.

The militia band struck up "Hail, Columbia!" and "Yankee Doodle." Then General Combs spoke, this time to a lively throng of 5,000 Kentuckians. When he concluded, according to custom, he invited any others to speak whom the people wished to hear. After a "long and unanimous call," Cassius Clay stood up and responded:

Men of Fayette. It is well-known to at least a portion of you, that no man has more steadily and unsparingly denounced this war than I. . . . Up to the time that this war was legalized by congressional assumption, it continued to meet my uncompromising opposition.

But now, stern necessity leaves me no alternative; my country calls for help, and, "right or wrong," I rally to her standard . . . .He shall be deemed the true friend of his country, who not only consistently warns her against evil, but rescues her from the danger of her errors or her crimes.

Then he concluded, "Now I fall into the ranks as a private, with my blanket and canteen," and stepped down into the deafening thunder of popular approval.

Clay in fact took his place in the ranks of the "Old Infantry," General Green Clay's original unit. It was common knowledge that proslavery politicians had intervened with Governor William Owsley to block Clay's appointment as colonel of a regiment, although he had held that rank in the state militia. Denied his command at Frankfort, "with some mortification of spirit," Clay returned to Lexington. He accepted his duty "with unshaken purpose," however, and started downtown to meet his unit.

Clay's friend, James S. Jackson, had been chosen captain of the Lexington Company. But Jackson called the company together at the courthouse, resigned his own captaincy, and nominated Clay in his place. Clay was unanimously elected. Even Mason Brown, son of the

Samuel M. Brown who fell to Clay's bowie knife at Russell's Cave Spring, voted for him. Both Jackson and Brown became lieutenants in the historic old unit, now mounted on fine Kentucky horses. Combining tradition with change, they called themselves the "Old Infantry Cavalry."

Clay's dramatic gesture shocked and pained a large number of his antislavery friends and subscribers, especially those in the North, but he knew what he was doing. His experiences at Russell's Cave and at the *True American* office had proved to him that he needed broader popular support than the advocacy of emancipation alone provided; he perceived that even some nonslaveholders had opposed him. He knew that Kentuckians were fond of military glory and he hoped that by taking part in the Mexican War he would strengthen himself so that, when he returned to take the stump against slavery again, he would be "an over-match for all my foes."

Politics aside, Clay was also patriotic. Resistance to his country's obligations, whether he approved them or not, he believed would be "true rebellion." Later, writing from Camargo, Mexico, in answer to abolitionist critics, he declared simply, "When I *spoke* against the Mexican War I said that I would *fight* it. I am here to redeem my pledge." Moreover, "I wished to *prove* to the people of the South that I warred not upon *them*, but upon *Slavery*, that a man might hate slavery and denounce tyrants without being the *enemy of his country*."

Colonel Humphrey Marshall, a graduate of West Point, was commandant of the Kentucky regiment. After weeks of delay in Louisville, the whole command was shipped to Memphis by steamer. To condition the troops, the officers then led the soldiers by land, crossing swamps, lagoons, and rivers to Little Rock, where they were feted. Clay's men cheered lustily as a lovely Arkansas belle presented their captain with a beautiful red ostrich feather, which Clay wore in his cap as the cavalry unit galloped out on the long trek to Port Lavaca on the Gulf.

Between the Nueces and the Rio Grande they saw great droves of wild horses, thick as migratory birds, racing across the plains, the noise of their passing "like the roar of a tornado."

By the time Clay was invited to meet General Taylor and his staff, "Old Rough and Ready" had already secured Monterrey. With Taylor's aide-de-camp, Colonel Bliss, and other officers, Clay shared the general's meal of salt pork, hardtack, and camp coffee served in tin cups. Although he found General Taylor "no politician," Clay observed that "my history was not unknown to him, and especially to Colonel Bliss." One of the officers with whom he spoke, for the first and only time, was General Taylor's son-in-law, Jefferson Davis.

Shortly thereafter Clay was detached from Marshall's regiment and under Major John P. Gaines was sent up the pass between the Sierra Madre and Mitre Mountain to Saltillo. There, under General William O. Butler's command, he advanced to the head of the column for scouting assignments. Rumors that Generalissimo Santa Anna, with an estimated 20,000 troops, was moving northward from San Luis Potosí required that the whole area south of Saltillo be reconnoitered.

On January 23, 1847, Major Solon Borland, Major Gaines, and their commands, including Captain Clay and the best men of his cavalry unit, were surrounded by over 3,000 Mexican troops and taken prisoners at the hacienda of Encarnacion. Borland was already encamped at the hacienda when Gaines arrived. Both majors ignored Clay's earnest protest against camping in the hacienda rather than in the open fields—"a course," Clay stated, "against all military rule and common sense." The commanders also failed to post the usual picket guards along approaching roads. Their negligence doomed the 71 men to capture.

When the sun burnt the fog from the plateau, the Americans found themselves surrounded by General

Miñon's regular Mexican cavalry. Crisis upon them, the majors forgot the contempt with which they had met Clay's entreaties for an encampment in the open plains, where, as Clay had said, they could "mount at once, and be ready for fight or flight." They hastened to Captain Clay for help; "surrendering the command" to him, as he later wrote, they "took places in the ranks."

Clay quickly computed the odds, "We stood less than one to forty-two of the enemy." The Americans had half as many rounds of shot as there were opposing foes. Their store of water was small, food for the men and forage for the horses almost nil. Not the remotest chance existed of reinforcement from Saltillo, about 110 miles away. They must somehow send back word of the enemy's approach. Although 3,000 Mexican troops waited to massacre the 71 Americans, Clay determined with his men either to exact honorable terms of "capitulation," or to "sell our lives like men who held the faith that honor is the only necessity." To achieve the former, it was clear that the surrounded cavalrymen must negotiate from a deceptively strong position.

Clay barricaded the doors of the hacienda and placed his men behind parapets and upon the roof. He ordered pavements torn up and carried aloft to serve as missiles. Then he stood, pistol in hand, his upper body exposed, to receive the advancing carabineers. Through the arrangement of his men, he kept their small numbers and comparative weakness a mystery to the lead officer, Colonel Mendoza. *"Arista!"* shouted the advancing Mexicans. *"Arista!"*

"Alamo!" Clay thundered in return, believing that "the Mexicans very well knew that Alamo meant no surrender, but war to the death." Meanwhile, Clay held the colonel, who had approached the front gate, within the sights of his pistol.

At once Colonel Mendoza ordered an officer to raise the white flag of parley. The result was a treaty that saved the lives of the Americans, respected what little property they had, except for weapons and horses (only the two majors were allowed to keep their personal mounts), and assured their Mexican guide a fair trial in the civil court. Later, Clay stated that he and his men "held General Miñon and [3,000] regular and veteran troops, as numbered by himself, at bay, from dawn till noon of the 23rd day of January."

The Lieutenant Cruset who later rode guard with "Señor Clayo" proved to be a Spanish Catholic who had also attended the College of Saint Joseph in Bardstown. Through him Clay learned that Colonel Mendoza was impressed with his gallant conduct of the defense. To honor him "with true old-time Spanish magnanimity," the Mexican officer provided Clay with one of his best Mexican horses.

Clay's quick thinking soon again averted slaughter. Among the American officers was Captain Dan Drake Henrie, who feared that he would be recognized by the Mexicans as an escaped prisoner from a defeated Texas expedition before the war. Henrie exchanged his Mexican horse for Major Gaines's faster American mount and asked advice of Clay, who agreed that Henrie's life was in great peril. "I told him I should be glad for our friends to know of the advance of the [Mexican] army," but in an affair of so much danger he did not urge escape upon the man. He also warned Henrie to "speak low," for he knew the Mexican lieutenant understood English. It was during this conference that Henrie's escape occurred, for the Mexican officer did, indeed, understand the conversation and immediately rode ahead to report it to the new commander of the prisoners, Colonel Zambonino. Suspecting that the Mexicans were making preparations to execute him, and seeing Borland and Gaines already ordered ahead under a heavy guard, Henrie left Clay and rode down the ranks under the pretense of closing them. He rode through eighty startled Mexican lancers, too, and then put spurs to his Kentucky horse, quickly distancing his pursuers.

Infuriated, Colonel Zambonino ordered the prisoners lanced, and the Mexicans promptly began backing their mounts far enough to gather momentum for the charge. During this maneuver, Clay, who was about twenty yards in front of the prisoners, quickly rode back to his men and commanded them to lie down and show no resistance—which they immediately did. Then Clay did an extraordinary thing, to which his men later attested. Standing in front of his prostrate men, Clay exclaimed: *"Kill the officers; spare the soldiers!"* In the excitement, the Mexican colonel then ordered three of the soldiers to lance Clay. But seeing order again restored, the Mexicans hesitated, even as they rode up—"one at each side and one in the rear." Thinking Clay responsible for the escape, Zambonino held an immense horse pistol to Clay's breast, while Cruset threatened him with a saber. With Zambonino's cocked pistol at his breast, he still exclaimed, *"Kill me—kill the officers; but spare the men—they are innocent!"*

Vainglorious as this action may seem, its courage struck the Mexican commander with admiration. "Seeing that the soldiers were safe, as they began to tie them," Clay later said, "I was not slow in talking in my own defense." Clay said that he knew of Henrie's "design to escape," but that he had not advised him to do so; that Henrie "had a right to act independently," and that "there was no intention to rise upon the guard." Zambonino countermanded his order. Clay lived, his men survived, and the escaped Henrie's information helped General Taylor achieve the crucial victory at Buena Vista one month later.

Before many days, the prisoners met Santa Anna's army marching northward from San Luis Potosí. When Clay saw his carriage, drawn by six horses "with postillions and outriders in great style," he could not help musing on Zachary Taylor "and his tin cups." The American officers gave the generalissimo little information, and he passed on to his defeat at Buena Vista.

The prisoners, following Santa Anna's previous route, went on to San Luis Potosí, where they were kept under guard for a few weeks. There, an Englishman entered their compound. "Is Mr. Clay among the prisoners?" he asked.

Clay said, "That is my name."

"Cassius M. Clay?"

"Yes."

"Did I not hear you speak in the Tabernacle, in New York City, in the year 1844?"

"I spoke there," Cassius said, not in a very pleasant humor. The Englishman retired but soon sent Clay and the others a cold leg of mutton stuffed with garlic, upon which they "feasted with great avidity."

On the resumed march south to Mexico City, the hungry prisoners were often reduced to eating dog or mule meat. Occasionally, however, women from the ranches and small villas charitably ran out with eggs, beans, and tortillas to relieve their hunger. People of the cities were less kind. At Querétaro the mob rose against "*Los Barbaros del Norte*" and stoned them. The prisoners ran into a cathedral, horses and all, upon order of the officers, and were saved by the asylum of sanctuary.

In Mexico City the Yankees were quartered in the monastery of Saint Jago, which had been converted into a state prison. Once a prisoner, Clay believed that all chance for military fame and glory perished. "Nothing was left me but the ever faithful discharge of duty," he remarked. In duty, though, he found himself declared "the soldier's friend," not on fields where armies struggled, nor in the proffer of his life to save the lives of his men, but in the compounds with his company. Though ill himself, poisoned by the lead pipes that bore the water from the main aqueduct, he managed to care for his sick and suffering men. Already he had shared his mount, turn by turn with them, so that they could stand the long march south, sometimes "forty miles a day," as they later said. Alert to their needs, he gained every privilege for them allowed by their captors. He "divided the last cent of money he had with us," they attested. When necessary, he disposed of his mount, and in order to supply the wants of his men, he sold "his buffalo rug, his watch, and all his clothes but one suit," and "expressed his regret that he was unable to do more."

By August 1847, General Scott had drawn within sight of the capital of the Republic, and the prisoners were removed to Toluca, the capital of the state of Mexico. Though only a long day's journey by horseback from Mexico City, to Clay, Toluca seemed "as far away as if it were a thousand miles." He described it as "the Arcadia of the ancient's imagination," with delicious food cooked over charcoal fires, an abundance of oranges, figs, lemons, bananas, and a climate of "perpetual spring." After months of incarceration within the gloomy prison walls of Mexico City, Toluca was a place where "the flow of the blood through the veins and arteries—existence itself—was a positive pleasure . . . and every sense was responsive to all lovely Nature." Which, it seems, included a lovely Tolucan girl of eighteen, whose auburn hair was "the fullest and longest I ever saw." Clay's memory of the Tolucan Lolu was rueful. A cat had eaten her pet parrot. All that she clutched of its life was a handful of bright feathers:

I never saw her look so interesting before; but so it is that, with or without art, they ever hold us the more firmly, the more they seem to be least thoughtful of our capture. Was this emblematic of our ever-drifting life; our sunshine and shade? when the most real joys fading into the dead past, leave us but rose-tinted memories of the days which are gone,—of the scenes which come no more, and whose only traces are—tears! . . . Poor Lolu!

By September 8, General Scott had captured Churubusco and Molino del Rey. When Chapultepec fell, his way to Mexico City lay unobstructed, and by mid-September, the Stars and Stripes waved over the capital of the Republic of Mexico. In Toluca, Clay went to Governor Oliguibel and protested further detention. Realizing that peace negotiations were already under way, Oliguibel gave the captain and his men an escort to General Scott. They were exchanged for Mexican prisoners—"many officers and men," Cassius noted, "whom Scott was too happy to turn loose."

Though he was released in late September, Clay's return to New Orleans was delayed. During the weeks that intervened he took in the sights of Mexico City, where he had been so long a captive. General Scott invited him to dinner and, after a pleasant conversation, asked him to deliver "words of *souvenir*" to John Speed Smith, Clay's brother-in-law, who believed with many others that Scott would be a prominent candidate for the presidency in the next election.

On Saturday, December 11, 1847, Cassius Clay arrived in Lexington by way of Frankfort, where Mary Jane had gone to meet him; now there were six children, ranging in age from the twelve-year-old Elisha to the nine-month-old infant Brutus, whom Clay had never seen. It had been little more than two years since the mob had risen against the *True American.* Yet the captain received a hero's welcome. Cannons boomed as he entered the city, and thousands of citizens cheered him along his way. The *Lexington Intelligencer* reported that "Kentucky's fair daughters . . . waved their handkerchiefs in token of their welcome." Military companies escorted the Clays to the Fayette County courthouse, while church bells pealed merrily over the city and "made the welkin ring."

Robert S. Todd gave the address of welcome. Several Mexican War veterans testified in public to "the valorous deeds of *our Cassius*," as a reporter enthusiastically noted. Further, these statements came not from "public functionaries," but from soldiers "who were eye-witnesses to his martial deeds." According to the *Observer*,

Clay responded "in appropriate and feeling terms." Overwhelmed with the reception, he invited everyone—about 500 people—to a collation that had been arranged at his home that evening. Fortunately his friends had made preparations. They illuminated the large lawn that fronted his Lexington residence and the party went on into the night.

Clay discovered that he had just missed meeting Robert Todd's son-in-law and seeing Mary again. Abraham Lincoln had been in Lexington visiting at the Todds' residence on West Main Street for the previous month of November. He had left by the Maysville stage with his family on Thanksgiving Day to go to Congress.

As Clay had publicly insisted before his departure to the war, his views on slavery remained unchanged. He continued to blame the Democratic administration for the Mexican War and its inefficient conduct. Determinedly, he set out in the spring of 1848 to defeat the Democrats, and he began by doing all in his power to procure the Whig nomination for Zachary Taylor over Henry Clay. As he stated in his speech at Richmond, Kentucky, on February 7, "When I go into the Presidential canvass I want to *win*." Clay did not want his champion "tied hand and foot and shorn of his strength." He frankly believed that Henry Clay had compromised too much and was too dependent on old party hacks, "who have life estates in *particular men*." Part of Clay's strategy was also to defeat the old-line Whigs who had "struck hands with the Democrats in the overthrow of the *True American*." He sued the Committee of Sixty for damages and recovered a judgment of $2,500. Horace Greeley commented that "the Freedom of the Press stands fully vindicated and established. Of the struggle, which has resulted thus auspiciously, the hero is Cassius M. Clay."

But of more importance were Clay's long-range plans to build up a new party of "universal liberty." He believed that Taylor's comparatively more independent position, as well as his popularity as a war hero, would cause support to gravitate to him. By and large, Clay's views proved correct. But as soon as Taylor received the nomination at Baltimore, Clay was filled with regret at the defeat he had dealt his kinsman and began to mend his fences with Gallant Harry, publicly admitting the error of his own rash actions in the past in straining their friendship.

By 1849 Clay was a leader in the state Liberal party—an organization of emancipationists, nonslaveholding and slaveholding, who hoped to elect antislavery delegates to the state constitutional convention held that year. Many of the gradualists opposed open discussion of the explosive slavery issue, believing it would weaken their position. But Clay rose in support of agitating the slavery question, and his views carried.

"We want men on the stump," he declared. Heeding his own advice, he made a trip to Lawrenceburg, Kentucky. He knew well that public discussion of slavery was more dangerous than debate in the press. Several citizens of Lawrenceburg called upon him and warned him that he was looked upon as an "incendiary" and that if he spoke it would be "at his own peril." But he believed that the arguments of emancipation had to reach the ears of the people.

Well it was that Clay's resolve was powerful, for when he got to the courthouse, he had to make his way through a hostile crowd. He had been careful to place his two revolvers near the mouth of his carpetbag and to conceal his bowie knife in his belt. As he advanced, a lane opened. The crowd was sullen, and no one said a word. The faces appeared, he thought, "excited and pale, as men who are on the eve of action." He moved on to the lectern.

In this instance, he was rescued by a giant of a Mexican War veteran named Wash, who began by saying that Captain Clay was a faithful friend to the soldier and declared that "the man who fights for the country has a right to speak about the country." And his "forty children and grandchildren" were there to "stand by Clay, or die!"

But Clay was not so fortunate at Foxtown on June 15, hardly two months later. Feeling safe because the speechmaking was on the Lexington-Richmond turnpike, hardly a mile from White Hall, he had neglected to bring his pistols in his hand-sack; he had only his bowie knife. He spoke standing on a table. When he stepped down, Cyrus Turner, the son of the proslavery candidate, shouted that Clay was lying and struck him. Clay drew his knife but was immediately surrounded by about twenty men. His arms were seized and his knife wrested from him. Surprised, and thinking the action could be a friendly intervention to avoid bloodshed, he made little resistance. But then the conspirators closed in, striking him with clubs. Clay was stabbed in the right lung, and the blow severed his breastbone. Knowing now he was to be murdered, Clay surged into the midst of the conspirators and grasped his bowie knife by the handle and blade. In retrieving his weapon, he cut two of his fingers to the bone. Additional blows fell upon his back, his kidneys, his pelvis.

The blood gushed violently from his chest while on the horn haft of his knife, the lacerated flesh of his fingers gave way to bone. Somehow, he found Cyrus Turner. Burning with pain and fury, Clay flourished the knife. The way opened. Clay advanced. The thrust of his hand found the man's abdomen, and the blade sank to the crosspiece. Fourteen-year-old Warfield Clay handed his father a pistol, but it was too late. He was already losing consciousness. Another member of the Turner clan ran up, held a pistol to Clay's head, and snapped it several times, but the percussion caps did not explode. Clay's friends reached him as he fainted away, crying out, "I died in the defense of the liberties of the people."

The next day, June 16, 1849, the *Lexington Observer*

reported, "Gentlemen who witnessed the conflict, state that Mr. Clay is dead," and added that Cyrus Turner was "not expected to recover." Indeed, as he suffered back into consciousness, everyone thought Clay would die—everyone except Clay himself. "I allowed no probing of the wound . . . relying on my vigor of constitution, and somewhat upon my destiny." It was Cyrus Turner who died.

7

AD ASTRA...

CLAY WAS SLOW to recover. His chest wound and the effects of the bludgeons upon his spine and pelvis caused occasional pain for the rest of his life. Dictating from his bed once again, Clay attempted to correct exaggerated and sometimes altogether untrue reports of the encounter at Foxtown. Just as the death of Cyrus Turner brought sympathy and support to the proslavery forces in Kentucky, Clay's bloody defense of his life was denounced throughout the East by Garrisonian abolitionists who advocated nonresistance. "And thus through life," he observed, "I have been between two fires—the Slavepower on one side, and the Abolition cranks on the other."

Although emancipation candidates polled thousands of votes all over Kentucky, they were not to elect a single delegate to the constitutional convention. When he could rise, Clay met "that infamous [1849] Constitution" with indignation. He ridiculed the arrogance of the slaveholder for attempting to secure perpetual rights to "his slave and the increase," and for holding such rights "higher than any other human or divine law!" He heaped contempt upon perpetualists who had ignored the rights of the people in a rank attempt to draft "an unchangeable Constitution."

By the spring of 1850, Clay was well enough to scorch

the columns of Washington's *Natural Era* with five blistering attacks upon Daniel Webster's famous March 7 speech in support of compromise. He was especially outraged about the Fugitive Slave Bill. One part of Henry Clay's last desperate compromise to hold secession-minded states within the Union, the measure required federal authorities and even the people of free states themselves, under threat of heavy fine and imprisonment, to cooperate with slaveowners in arresting and returning escaped slaves to the states from which they had fled. Clay forecast the storm of protest that swept through the North and scorned Webster's lapse of leadership: "It is a source of regret to all lovers of American genius, that you did not prove as gloriously great, as you are unquestionably talented!"

Determined to attack Whiggery, Clay ran for governor on the Emancipation ticket in 1851. Campaigning strenuously throughout the summer, he realized that he could not win, but he was determined to destroy the Whig party in Kentucky and drive its membership, as now seemed necessary, toward an antislavery stance with the North and West and with the liberals of the East. Only in this way, he believed, could the proslavery Democrats of both South and North—and such atrocities as the Fugitive Slave Law and slavery itself—ultimately be defeated. Clay received about 5,000 votes, and satisfied himself that he kept as many as 30,000 people from the polls in silent protest against the now-compromised Whig ticket. The upshot was that Lazarus Powell, the Democratic candidate, was elected by a thin plurality of less than 1,000 votes. Clay proclaimed his triumph in the old party's defeat: "Thus, and forever, fell the Whig Party in Kentucky."

In order to pass the Kansas-Nebraska Bill of 1854, which in effect allowed both proposed territories to "vote slavery up" or "vote slavery down" by the constitutions they chose to adopt, it was necessary to repeal the old Missouri Compromise of 1820, which prohibited slavery north of 36° 30′ latitude. The Kansas-Nebraska Bill also called for more stringent enforcement of the 1850 Fugitive Slave Law. The antislavery forces of the North were aroused to see slavery expansionists of the South about to have their way. The result among the Whigs was increased division. After the repeal of the Missouri Compromise, Clay believed that "slavery and liberty could no longer co-exist" as principles within the same political party or, indeed, within the same nation. Once again Clay saw farther than most of his contemporaries, for the destruction of the Whigs in Kentucky augured the old party's national demise in 1860. As the breach widened between North and South, the choice became increasingly clear: either the voters would turn to proslavery Democrats, or they would join a new party that would curb extension of slavery into federal territory.

As a powerful antislavery advocate, Clay was invited to speak throughout the North. During one of these lecture tours, on July 10, 1854, he was scheduled to address an audience at Springfield, Illinois, but he was denied the use of the State House. Instead, he spoke to about 1,500 people from a hastily constructed platform in a grove near a Mrs. Mather's residence, some distance from the city square. His chief purpose was to "stigmatize" the aggression of the South in the "Nebraska and Kansas outrage." Concerning slavery itself, he determined to "strike at the monster aggressor whenever it could be reached under the Constitution," through an organization of men of "whatever politics, of Free Soilers, Whigs, and Democrats, who will . . . unite in hurling down the gigantic evil which threatens even our liberties." It was a spirited crowd that met Clay, and some carried their spirits in quarts.

"Would you help a runaway slave?" one heckler shouted.

"That depends on which way he was running," Clay shot back. He carried his point in a gale of laughter. Clay spoke vigorously for two and one-half hours. The next day, the *State Journal* praised it as "a Great Heroic Speech. . . . He spoke boldly, proudly, his sentiments—in the face and eyes of all the contumely and insults thrown upon him. . . . C. M. Clay [has] made several speeches in different parts of the state. We believe he has been, in every place with the exception of this, respectfully treated."

Abraham Lincoln was in the crowd that heard the speech. Clay was later to recall that Lincoln and his associate, Orville H. Browning, were under the trees. "Whittling sticks, as he lay on the turf, Lincoln gave me a most patient hearing. I shall never forget his long, ungainly form, and his ever sad and homely face."

Clay believed that the words he spoke on such occasions as this, as well as his articles in the Lexington and Louisville newspapers, were "like seed sown in good ground." And he was not thinking of Lincoln only, for ultimately, when the crisis came in 1861, the loyal element of Kentucky "stood impregnable for the Union of our fathers." Later, when Clay and Lincoln were on their way to New York City to speak before the Young Men's Republican Union, they renewed their friendship. Inevitably their conversation turned to slavery, "the great issue," upon which Clay talked while Lincoln listened, as Clay himself reported. "He listened a long time—such was his habit—without saying a word; and, when I had concluded my argument, he replied: 'Yes, I always thought, Mr. Clay, that the man who made the corn should eat the corn.' "

Other men—"weak men," as Clay observed—thought Lincoln lowered himself with such commonplace aphorisms. But Clay, possibly remembering how his own father had taught him, thought of the style of Franklin. To him Lincoln was "natural and robust, and therefore impressive and convincing." While such an educated man as Charles Sumner would object to Lincoln's description of a disloyal person as a "bad egg," Clay thought "those two words expressed more than ordinary men could put in many sentences."

Meanwhile, Clay had carried on an extended correspondence with John G. Fee, a crusading abolitionist preacher, whose *Antislavery Manual* (1848) had attracted Clay's attention. Through Clay's influence, Fee was invited to southern Madison County, first in 1853, to speak to mountain men who owned no slaves and stood for freedom. Here in the foothills of the Cumberlands, Clay owned a tract of land known as the "glade." Too long he had seen the mountain people, unable to compete against the slavery system, "bulldozed" by the slave power and "starved" into emigration to Ohio, Indiana, and the West. "So," he determined, "I set about finding a remedy for this exhausting evil." Specifically, he wished to establish a community of nonslaveholders. "I projected a school of education for their benefit," he wrote, and "I saw in Fee's heroic and pious character a fit man for the service I projected." Responding to Clay's call, Fee willingly came from Bracken County on the Ohio River in northern Kentucky, and agreed to undertake the work.

Clay gave Fee a ten-acre portion of the "glade" for a homestead, on which the pioneering abolitionist built his house. Fee called the land Berea, after the place in the New Testament where the apostle Paul found the people "open-minded." Under the date of March 29, 1855, Clay's diary contains the entry: "Paid John G. Fee $200 in full of contribution to his house." By the next year, Fee's church-school that was to become Berea College had made a good start. Years later, Clay declared that he had not foreseen Berea's rapid growth in educating young people without regard to race, caste or sex. Of Berea he said, "We builded better than we knew." Of the "patriotic and Christian work" itself, he acknowledged that the honor "belongs to John G. Fee alone."

During these years, commencing with the failure of his

Cincinnati Bank in late 1854, Clay suffered severe financial reverses, but he still managed to support Fee's dedicated work. By 1856 Clay's finest possessions, including his library and various objets d'art, were placed on the auction block at White Hall for public sale. His wealthy father-in-law, Dr. Elisha Warfield, made no effort to help Cassius and Mary Jane during this crisis. The result was to strain further the family relationship. Fortunately, Clay's mother and his brother Brutus bought in most of his property and transferred the debt to themselves, assigning the property to him.

Further, in the summer of 1855 when Fee was violently driven from Crab Orchard in Lincoln County where he was speaking against slavery, Clay reasoned, "If we were not allowed to speak freely according to our constitutional rights, our whole scheme for emancipation failed." So he made an appointment to speak on slavery in the same place himself. "It was necessary," he explained, "to set my life upon the cast of the die." And there he went, surrounded with armed followers, and "took the ground." Clay also spoke at Stanford, following Fee's ouster—"for our strength was a moral strength," and "if I spoke with safety," the slavery power's "policy of intimidation was broken forever."

According to legend, Clay always walked alone down the center aisle of the courtroom or meeting house, carrying his carpetbag. He mounted the dais and faced the hostile crowd. "For those who obey the rules of right, and the sacred truths of the Christian religion," he would say, as he held a Bible aloft, "I appeal to this Book"—and he would place it on the speaker's table. "To those who respect the laws of this country," he would announce, taking a copy of the Constitution out of his bag, "this is my authority"—and so saying, set the book down by the Bible. "But to those who recognize only the law of force—" (here he would bring forth two long-barrelled pistols, thumping them down on the table in front of him, and draw his bowie knife, which he held so that the blade caught the light before he dropped it casually on his brace of pistols) "for those—here is my defense!"

This legend is treasured in central Kentucky and perhaps has its seed of truth. But in later years it troubled the aging Clay, who took exception to such accounts. He meant no such "prepared and threatened exhibition of my courage and prowess," he contended. Indeed, had he laid a weapon on the bookboard, he pointed out, "some enemy was most likely to seize it." Nor did he wish any sensational action to kindle a conflagration, which would only have defeated his purpose. "I had my carpetbag with my arms and notes, as usual, at my feet, unseen, and the Bible on the board was always left there in the country meeting-houses." Recounting the Stanford story, however, Clay commented, "The excitement was intense, but I was heard without a single interruption."

Despite all his problems and reversals, by 1856 Clay was active in the new Republican party and was influential in its adoption of a strong antislavery platform. Clay was invited to the February meeting in Pittsburgh, the purpose of which was to arrange for the first Republican convention at Philadelphia, but he was not able to attend either meeting. He sent along a letter, however, read to the gathering by Michigan's Governor Kinsley Bingham. In response, one of the new leaders, George W. Julian, stated that Clay's "arraignment of slavery" was "impassioned and powerful," and that his voice even in absentia was a mighty aid in "guiding and inspiring" the Republicans, who might otherwise have adopted a more moderate stand on the issue. Clay campaigned vigorously for the 1856 Republican ticket of John C. Frémont and William L. Dayton, addressing immense audiences in the North. Between 1856 and 1860, he was a powerful, outspoken member of the Republican National Committee.

Clay began the 1860 campaign with an act of daring that unquestionably required all the strength of his convictions to subdue the fear any rational man would feel under similar circumstances. With only the frail light of a few lanterns to dispel the drizzling January darkness, he spoke for three hours from the portico of the capitol in Frankfort. "Whether I stand in your State House or whether I stand outside," he declared, "surrounded by light or covered by darkness, I feel equally safe while I am among Kentuckians." He proceeded then to denounce proslavery Democrats in fiery epithet, declare the consistency of his views, the price he had paid for them, and his hope for ultimate freedom:

I have stood by you all the long days of my youth and manhood, extinguished all the aspiration of ambition, suffered ignominy and contempt, been denounced, spurned and avoided by the men whose interests I was arguing. . . . but still holding myself true to one purpose, I stand there still. . . . Kentuckians, come war, come peace, I trust in God I may have the fortune to stay there during the rest of my days . . . however visionary . . . true to the banner which I would have float over us.

Clay reached a pinnacle of popularity the next month with a stunning address delivered at the Tabernacle of New York before the Young Men's Republican Central Committee. Soon thereafter, *Harper's Weekly* published a large spread of the likenesses of the major Republican candidates for nomination. New York's Seward was featured in the center with a view of Washington City just below. On the left of these were engraved the countenances of Edward Bates, William Pennington, Salmon Chase, Frémont, and Lincoln; and on the right, those of Nathanial Banks, John McLean, Simon Cameron, John Bell, and Cassius M. Clay.

Clay took great interest in the approaching convention at Chicago. At the outset, he stood neutral between Seward and Chase, for they were both his friends and, in his judgment, "equally qualified for office," but his opinion was soon to change. On a visit to Washington he dined with Seward, who showed him a speech in which Seward took the ground that he was "for the *Union, slave or free.*" Clay thought, "I did not see the necessity of making a great party, and a great to-do about slavery, if we were to end where we began." He said nothing to Seward, but "*it killed Seward with me forever!*" Moreover, Seward's "renowned camp-follower," Thurlow Weed, met Clay at Albany. In Clay's words, "Weed talked all I wanted," but when Clay presented him with a written proposal, "which would commit him and his friends, in case of Seward's defeat in Chicago, to me and my friends," the political manipulator made no reply. One gathers that Clay did not trust Seward and Weed; concerning the latter, he said, "I had no faith in this talk." Leaving Albany uncommitted, Clay observed, "From that day to the death of both these men, they were my implacable enemies."

After Chase had dropped out of the race, failing to receive the backing of his own Ohio delegation, he wrote Clay in essence what many Republicans believed: "You united elements of character, ability, and popularity which would make you an available candidate; whilst your early, continued, and devoted service to the cause gave you claims over the preference of your old co-laborers, which no true-hearted man could fail to appreciate." Although the Blairs at Silver Springs, Maryland, offered him the cabinet post of secretary of war in return for his support of Missourian Bates, Clay knew nothing of the respectable old Whig's principles and declined to support him. With national survival at stake, the Kentuckian was convinced of the "right to destroy slavery," and wrote that "it was my purpose to do so," believing "there could be no liberty, even for the whites, in coexistence with this barbarism."

Between Lincoln and Bates, Clay preferred Lincoln. Both Clay and Lincoln, at the invitation of the Young Men's Republican Union in New York, had made popular addresses at the Cooper Institute in February 1860. Perhaps Clay remembered Lincoln's convincing arguments for prohibition of slavery in the territories, and his ability to discuss the whole question of slavery in terms under-

79

standable to both the North and the South. Many possibilities remained open for Clay, had he been intent upon self-aggrandizement; but when all was said and done, he threw his considerable influence behind another native-born Kentuckian. Addison G. Proctor remembered Clay's persuasive eloquence as he spoke to the wavering Kansas delegation at their hotel:

"We are on the eve of a great civil war," began Mr. Clay, but we of Kansas were used to strong words and smiled. The Ketuckian looked at us sternly and continued:

"We know what your platform plans are and I am here to say that if a candidate is nominated on that platform the South will make an attempt to dissolve the Union. Your southern border extends from Maryland to Missouri and on this side stands a determined body of men, resolute that the Union shall not be destroyed except after a most desperate struggle.

"It makes a great difference to you whom you nominate," thundered on the tall Kentuckian, "and it makes a much more vital difference to us. Our homes and all we possess are in peril. We demand of you a candidate who will inspire our courage and confidence. We call upon you to nominate Abraham Lincoln, who knows us and understands our aspirations. Give us Lincoln and we will push back your battle line from the Ohio River to the Tennessee, where it belongs. Give us Lincoln and we will unite the strength of our Union sentiment with the Union army and bring success to your legions. Do this for us," pleaded the speaker, "and we will go home and prepare for the conflict."

We saw things from a new angle. It was no longer a question of fighting slavery, but of saving the Union. Lincoln was nominated.

Clay's decision seems to have been motivated by patriotism, for in going for Lincoln he virtually annihilated his own chances for the vice-presidential nomination on geographic grounds alone. "At one time," journalist Murat Halstead reported, "a thousand voices called Clay! Clay! to the convention. If the multitude could have had its way, Mr. Clay would have been put on the ticket by acclamation." Of the 233 votes required for a choice, on the first ballot Clay received 101½, but since Lincoln was the presidential nominee, "it was thought prudent," as Clay recognized, "to allow Seward's friends to name the Vice-President; and, Hamlin of Maine being a Northern man, and Seward's friend, it was also thought best to nominate him, and not me, of an adjoining State." Accordingly Hamlin received 194 votes on the first ballot, and the second put him over the top; it was Clay's floor manager who moved that the nomination be made unanimous. Later, Clay wrote, "It was generally talked of at Chicago, that I was to be made Secretary of War; and Lincoln himself wrote me to that effect." Moreover, during the campaign that followed, Clay was on the hustings at Lincoln's personal behest: "Still more will you oblige us," the candidate wrote from Springfield, "if you will allow us to make a list of appointments in our State, commencing, say, at Marshall, in Clark County, and thence South and West, along our Wabash and Ohio river border." Perhaps more than any one campaigner, Clay helped to carry Indiana, which was then Democratic, for Lincoln.

The day after Lincoln's election, protesting South Carolinians lowered the Stars and Stripes in Charleston and ran up the palmetto flag in its place. December 20, South Carolina led the exodus of seceding states. February 9, 1861, a month before Lincoln's inauguration day, the Confederate States of America formed a government at Montgomery, Alabama. In Charleston Harbor, Major Robert Anderson of Louisville refused for thirty-four hours to surrender square-walled Fort Sumter, gallantly directing the defense against the artillery fire of General P. G. T. Beauregard, who had received orders to reduce it to rubble if necessary.

Cassius Clay arrived in Washington in mid-April to find the capital seething with outrage at the defiance of South Carolina. Although several leading newspapers and organizations had endorsed Clay as secretary of war, Lincoln was committed to Simon Cameron. Clay went to the White House where he found the president in the library. Not reminding Lincoln at this time of "the promise about the War Department," as he had understood it, he spurned the announcement that he had been appointed minister plenipotentiary to Spain, saying that he "would not accept the mission to an old, effete government like Spain." Discovering that the posts at London and Paris had been filled, Clay later observed, "I saw the hand of Seward in all my defeats." He told Lincoln that he had labored for the time "when I could accept office only to vindicate my principles, but since you have so many better men than myself I think I had better go back to Kentucky and retire to private life."

"Lincoln, who had been rather reserved up to this time," as Clay remembered the incident, "here got up and put his hand on my shoulder and said: 'I don't want you to go home, Mr. Clay. I want to do something for you, but I am so hedged around here that I can't do just what I will. Isn't there some place you will take?' "

At a later conference at the White House, Clay settled on the Russian ministry with the new president. Lincoln rose and took the Kentuckian's hand, saying, "Clay, I thank you; you relieve me of great embarrassment."

However, Clay was not to proceed to Saint Petersburg without first encountering a nearer and more urgent duty. Even though Lincoln had declared a state of insurrection, Washington was riddled with secessionists, traitors, and would-be assassins. Troops of the Sixth Massachusetts Regiment on the way to the capital were attacked in the streets of Baltimore; blood was shed and bridges were fired. In desperation, Lincoln told a Maryland delegation, "I *must* have troops for the defence of the capital. The Carolinians are marching across Virginia to seize the capital and hang me. What am I to do? I *must* have troops, I say; and as they can neither crawl under Maryland nor fly over it, they must come across it." Obviously the capital city and Lincoln's life were imperiled. Under these circumstances, Clay sent his family—Mary Jane and all the children except Green, who had volunteered as a Union soldier—on to Philadelphia. He went directly to the War Department and offered his services in the defense of Washington to Secretary Simon Cameron "as an officer to raise a regiment, or as a private in the ranks."

The front page of the *New York Times* carried the story of Clay's offer. "I don't believe," Cameron said in mild surprise, "I ever heard of where a foreign Minister volunteered in the ranks."

"Then," said Clay, "let's make a little history."

As commander of the Clay Battalion, Clay guarded the Navy Yard, cleared the city of masses of southern sympathizers, and protected the White House until the Federal regiments arrived on the scene. President Lincoln issued an order expressing his gratitude to Clay and presented him with a Colt revolver as tangible testimony of his regard. Senator Charles Sumner, who distrusted West Point and the regular army, persistently urged Clay to accept the rank of major general, assuring him that Lincoln would make the appointment. Recognizing his professional limitations in military matters, however, Clay declined the "great honor" proffered him, but informed Sumner that "if it turned out that I was absolutely needed to give confidence to the Union army . . . [Lincoln] might recall me from Russia, and I would do my best to serve the country at home."

In accepting the Russian portfolio, Clay had formidable obstacles to overcome, not the least of them being the animosity of the new secretary of state, Seward himself. He "treated me," Clay noted, "with the greatest coolness." Yet with characteristic verve the new minister journeyed on undismayed to Saint Petersburg by way of London and Paris.

First on shipboard and then in London, Clay saw Lincoln's new minister to England, Charles Francis Adams, whose son Henry was to observe, "Secretary Seward had occasion to learn the merits of Cassius M. Clay in the diplomatic service, . . . Cassius Clay as a teacher having no equal though possibly some rivals." While Clay was in England, he learned that Arkansas and Tennessee had seceded and that Jefferson Davis had boldly moved his capital northward to Richmond; but the worst news for the diplomatic corps was that Queen Victoria had recognized the Confederates as belligerents—a first step, it appeared, toward recognizing their separate-nation status. Moreover, after dining with the prime minister, Clay perceived official England's desire for dissolution of the Union. He knew, of course, that the aristocracy would be happy to see the republic break into pieces, but he had faith in the great mass of middle and working class people, many of whom saw the South darkly—as pictured in Harriet Beecher Stowe's *Uncle Tom's Cabin*.

In this situation Clay could say what Lincoln could not, and what the cautious Adams could find no proper way of uttering. Cutting through all protocol, he wrote a letter to the *Times* appealing directly to the British people, reminding them of their hatred of slavery, their love of loyalty to country, and the wisdom of keeping a "natural ally" in the western world whose strength and friendship could prove a future salvation. Above all, to support the rebellion would be to support the evil of slavery; if their sympathies were with liberty, then their leaders would be *"wise"* to support the Union. "This letter," Clay believed, "did much to hold the British people from the hazardous alliance with France and the Mexican Invasion." However, this vigorous twisting of the British lion's tail displeased Seward's friend, Adams, as well as British officialdom, jealous of all rivalry on the sea and economically linked to the cotton interests of the South. Clay ignored all objections, believing "the whole letter . . . friendly and highly complimentary to the British Nation."

Clay was an immediate diplomatic success in Saint

Petersburg, but his first stint as minister to Russia lasted only about a year. When Cameron, as Clay put it, "got into bad odor" for his dealings with the railroads and the government, it was decided to send him to Russia. Clay was recalled and commissioned a major general. He returned to Washington in time to hear all about the humiliation of having Jeb Stuart and his rebel-yelling cavalry of 1,200 ride around the whole Army of the Potomac—150,000 men—striking at will, Stuart's black plume waving like an unanswered challenge. He also saw Federal troops pouring back into the capital. Now it seemed that another invasion of the North was imminent and that Washington itself was about to be threatened again, this time by Lee.

Clay remarked to Lincoln that the war certainly was "and ought to be a failure, with the old cancer of slavery left in the Union." He urged that it was long past time to declare the slaves "of all the States in rebellion free." His argument was consistent with his lifelong position on emancipation, but this time he added the force of diplomatic logic to his arguments with the president:

The autocracy of Europe were ready to destroy the great Republic, which was ever a menace to the crowned-heads. That whilst we fought simply for empire, the people of . . . England and France were indifferent to our success; but that, in the cause of liberty, we would have a safe check upon their rulers, who would not dare to interfere in behalf of slavery. . . . if fall we must, let us fall with the flag of universal liberty and justice nailed to the mast-head. Then, at least, we should have the help of God, and the sympathies of mankind, for a future struggle, and live in the memory of the good in all time.

Then Clay, though now commissioned a major general, requested that he be permitted to go back to Russia and do all in his power to keep the European powers out of the American war and to keep Russia solidly behind the Union.

85

"Lincoln listened with great attention," Clay observed. When the topic of conversation turned to the cabinet post of secretary of war, which Clay believed had been promised him, Lincoln felt obliged to respond to what Clay had considered an obligation. "Who ever heard of a reformer reaping the rewards of his work in his lifetime?" And he explained, "I was advised that your appointment as Secretary of War would have been considered a declaration of war upon the South." Lincoln then assured Clay that he would back him in his desire to return to the Court of Saint Petersburg if he wished.

But Clay did not let his points rest there with Lincoln. While in Washington, he was the house guest of Salmon Chase, now secretary of the treasury and one of Lincoln's chief critics. Clay drilled his points home to Chase, an antislavery advocate and intimate friend since 1835. "When I . . . saw how the war was going on, I began to think that, if I could carry on the war by declaring the slaves free, we could win; if not, we should fail." Chase agreed with Clay's sentiments and was extremely anxious that he should take a command, but the Kentuckian warned him that Edwin M. Stanton and Henry W. Halleck would place obstacles in his path. Further, Clay stated, "I had so told Lincoln . . . and . . . asked to return to St. Petersburg." Chase thought Clay might be mistaken. Through much of August, with Chase's personal help, Clay sought a command acceptable to him. Finally, after both Clay and Chase went to see a "very reserved" Halleck, even Chase was convinced that Clay could not expect fair play.

But Clay was not obliged to remain silent and did not do so. On August 12, he spoke to a large audience at the Odd Fellows' Hall in Washington. Cheering was vociferous as he built toward the climax of his speech. The correspondents of several major newspapers, including the *Cincinnati Gazette*, were there to pass on his remarks to the nation—and, of course, to Lincoln, an inveterate reader of newspapers:

"Well, now, you are going to conquer the South. How? By my friend Seward taking dinners and drinks? (*Laughter and applause*.) You are going to conquer the South by taking the sword in one hand and slave-shackles in the other. You are going to conquer the South with one portion of your force, while the other is detailed to guard rebel property. . . . How long have you tried it? For nearly eighteen months. Some of the best men in this country have gone down to their graves. Two hundred and fifty thousand of the loyal troops of the United States have died on the battle-field, or been disabled by sickness. How many millions have you expended? Why, a sum rolling up to one thousand millions—almost one-fourth of the national debt of England, that has been accumulating for ages. . . . Upon such principles as those you can not stand upright in the eye of the world. . . . Gentlemen, how much longer is this thing to continue?

"Fight this war on the principle of common-sense. As for myself, never, so help me God, will I draw a sword to keep the chains upon another fellow-being." (*Tremendous applause*.)

Lincoln was not long in sending for Clay. "I have been thinking of what you said to me, but I fear if such proclamation of emancipation was made Kentucky would go against us; and we have now as much as we can carry."

Clay replied, "You are mistaken. The Kentuckians have heard this question discussed by me *for a quarter of a century;* and have all made up their minds. Those who intend to stand by slavery have already joined the rebel army; and those who remain will stand by the Union at all events."

Lincoln then said, "The Kentucky Legislature is now in session. Go down, and see how they stand, and report to me."

So Clay set out at once. In Lexington, with the Battle of Richmond imminent, he aided General Lew Wallace in advancing raw, new troops toward the Kentucky River, but he was relieved by General William Nelson before battle. Clay then went on to Frankfort on August 27, and there addressed the legislature. As the president's special emissary, he was well received. Upon his return to Washington, he reported to Lincoln that the loyal element of Kentucky would hold and support a program of emancipation which protected their property interests. Clay handed Lincoln a copy of his speech (published in the *Cincinnati Gazette*, August 31) and completed his verbal report "of my visit to the State of Kentucky and the Kentucky Legislature." In response, as Clay recalled, "Lincoln said but little." The following weeks, however, proved eventful. Lincoln waited until the Union victory of Antietam to release, on September 22, the Emancipation Proclamation.

During the nights that followed, Washington was in a festive mood. In jubilation great crowds serenaded in turn Lincoln, Chase, and Clay.

Clay's joy may have been bittersweet. He had set out in life one of the wealthiest men in the West, but he had long ago directed his energies and means primarily to the accomplishment of his great purpose. Though he loved his family, his ambition and his duties had kept him from them often—speaking engagements, political campaigns, the Mexican War, the Saint Petersburg post, and now the Civil War. A dark cloud of debt had moved over him since the 1850s, and for a long time now, his relations with Mary Jane and the Warfields had been strained. Clay's face was still handsome but now bore the lines of a hard life; his figure still was erect and strong. His thick dark hair was streaked with gray. Now, as he looked down at the celebrators, he thought of Lincoln's official measure as "the culminating act of my life's aspirations."

He later wrote in simple eloquence, "Thus my good star stood high in the heavens."

8

CLAY OF THE WHITE NIGHTS: RUSSIA

AT A GRAND BALL in Saint Petersburg, Cassius Clay appeared in the uniform of a major general. Upon his broad shoulders bullion epaulets and stars shimmered under the pure white light of sconces tiered with burning wax candles. The pier glass reflected a room alive with the beau monde of Russia, many of them Clay's friends—the Davidoffs, the Apraxines, the Koucheleffs, Count Stroganoff, who had married the emperor's sister, and many others. Clay wore a jewel-encrusted sword at his waist and a silver scabbard containing what he jokingly referred to as his "dress-up bowie-knife." The courtiers had been most curious about his celebrated "duellos" in the distant Republic, and he wore it because he did not wish to disappoint them. But he seldom spoke of his violent encounters in public, and because he did not seem especially proud of them, no braggadocio was attributed to him.

"I thought my first duty in Russia was to keep the Czar on the Union side," Clay wrote, "and, therefore, my business was to *please*." He made it a rule to study every rank in Russian society, and he took pains to associate with the first families of Russia. Clay's few elegant entertainments, absorbing much of his salary during the first years of his ministry, impressed the Russians. "If they liked flowers," Clay said, "I accommodated them; if paintings, I had invested in some of the rarest; if wines, I had every sample of the world's choice; if the *menu* was the object, nothing was there wanting." His aristocratic origins and training combined with a refreshing social presence and natural friendliness to make the handsome Kentuckian's invitations much sought after, as he, himself, was much in social demand. He belonged to every major club in Saint Petersburg and made many friendships, both personal and political—an achievement that went far beyond conventional or official duties.

In so doing, Clay was fulfilling Seward's instructions, doubtless reviewed by Lincoln. The minister's primary responsibility was to gain the sympathy and support of the Russian Empire for the Union. Clay's letter in the *Times* to the British people had attracted attention throughout Europe, as had his Paris speech in 1861, a year of crop failures all over Europe that made northern grain of more value to Europe than southern cotton. Exposing the myth of King Cotton, Clay had declared "*Le cotton est Roi dit-on non. C'est le blé qui regne!*" The remark had long ago filtered through the French-speaking court of Saint Petersburg. Clay had, it was widely believed, done much to hold the British people from an alliance with Napoleon and involvement in the Mexican invasion. The Russians were Anglophobes, so they were delighted.

So successful was the first phase of his mission to Saint Petersburg that, when Clay left for Washington in 1862, his departure was surrounded by both official and personal disappointment. Alexander Mikhailovich Gortchacow, then foreign minister and later chancellor, asked Colonel Charles De Arnaud, while taking his hand: "I beg you to convey to the President of the United States on behalf of His Majesty and the Russian people, our hearty sympathy for maintenance of the Union. . . . Also, I beg of you to say to the President, to use his influence with Mr. Clay to remain with us, for his knowledge aids us a great deal and especially as he is liked not only by his Imperial Majesty but by all those with whom he comes in contact." Even the reluctant Seward was so impressed by Clay's evocation of "active, profound and unalterable sympathies for the Union" from the emperor himself, and his hope that it should be restored to "its ancient glory," that he told former Secretary of War Cameron, who temporarily had replaced Clay, "The [parting] speech made by Mr. Clay was so just in its expression of the sentiments of the President and the American people and the reply of his Majesty was so generous and faithful that . . . the whole transaction is regarded with the highest satisfaction by the government. . . . I cannot refrain from expressing, as [Clay] returns to us to exchange diplomacy for the sterner duties of the field that he will leave little for his successor to do."

The Russians also knew that while Seward had not insisted upon emancipation as a condition for restoration of the Union, Clay had done so with characteristic fearlessness and conviction. He had asserted his views to Lincoln himself as well as to the people of Washington and the Republic. What he lacked in the finer edges of the diplomatic image, he more than made up in the force of his personality. As one commentator noted, Clay did not "always measure with nice exactness his words." Rather, his noble sense of right and indignation at wrong, "flowed out in burning words like a pent-up Vesuvius." Such was the effect of his 1863 Albany speech, translated into Russian and widely circulated, with the approval of Alexander II, upon Clay's return to Saint Petersburg. He dramatically correlated the Emancipation Proclamation and its effects with foreign relations: "Whatever may be the feelings of foreign aristocracies against Republicanism, the liberals of all Europe are for the principles of freedom and Emancipation. Whilst the People of England are secured to us by the Proclamation, the Government dare not intervene on the side of slaveholders.

Russia is with us on the basis of common interests. . . . As much as the liberation of slaves is a *war measure*, yet far more is it a peace measure. If you would have peace be just; for justice is the only peace."

Strangely enough, at the very time of Clay's secret mission for Lincoln in Kentucky, when the Union victory at Antietam was still on the horizon, England's leaders were about to intervene in the Civil War. In the words of Lord Russell, "The time is come for offering mediation to the United States Government with a view to the recognition of the independence of the Confederates." France, of course, would be expected to participate in arranging "the basis of separation."

But Antietam followed, and Lee was driven back into Virginia. The Emancipation Proclamation was released just at that moment, bringing into the proposed negotiations a moral element the innate force of which Cassius Clay, perhaps more than any other American, had anticipated. Meanwhile, Gortchacow had instructed Baron Brunnow, the Russian ambassador to England, "Russia has no intention of changing her policy of extreme friendship to the United States." The president let Lord Russell know through Adams in London that European interference would mean war, and that England should "leave the struggle to settle itself." In the continuing European quest for an "armistice" between North and South, Russia did not participate. Clay had done his work well.

So completely was the cause of the Confederacy put down in England that its commissioner, James M. Mason, left in disgust. The Russians were delighted with the turn of events. When Clay returned to Saint Petersburg, he found the attitude of the whole diplomatic corps changing. Before, the European governments had thought the cause of the Union lost, and in Clay's view, "they could not conceal their satisfaction." But in 1863, after emancipation and after the victories of Meade, Grant, and Rosecrans, they were markedly more tolerant, if not always friendly.

Just as Russia had stood by the Union in its darkest hours, the Republic stood by Russia during the crisis of the Polish Insurrection. Clay gained both moral and substantive support for Russia from his own country. As the winter of 1863–1864 approached, Russia was threatened with war by England, France, and Austria. Clay wrote Seward: "Russia fortifies, she will not be bullied."

The Russian fleet set out on a cruise that brought it to the safer, ice-free harbors of the United States. The fleet under command of Admiral Lessoffsky was welcomed into New York by October 1, while Rear Admiral Popoff cruised the north Pacific. Clay observed that most European powers considered these moves to indicate a Russo-American alliance. "Many attempts were made to sound me upon this subject," Clay stated, "but I looked wise and said nothing."

Informed in the summer of 1864 of a proposed peace conference, Clay rejoiced that "the President has consented to make peace with the South upon the basis, only, of a restoration of the Union and the abolition of slavery." Yet he was not surprised that the Hampton Roads Peace Conference of the following February came to nothing, except "in exposing the ingratitude of the South toward their virtual allies, France and England." He went further in commenting on the South, writing to Seward, on March 1, 1865, "In no case would they accept Mr. Lincoln's clemency. I know the South better than you. Sherman and Grant are the peace makers."

But when Richmond fell, Clay wrote to a friend, "I join in your aspiration, for peace with all the world. Let us pardon our enemies at home and abroad with undeserved magnanimity. . . . If we should be compelled to make a stern example of some of the leaders of the rebellion, let the people feel that we are as capable of mercy as we are terrible in vengeance in arms."

After Lee's surrender to Grant, Clay was filled with the exhilaration of victory. In a style reminiscent of his antislavery stump speeches, he wrote, "I thank God that He bares His right arm in our cause, in vindication of justice and benevolence." The legations that had held aloof from the Union changed their manner. "Even across the street," Clay observed, "they would raise their hats!"

With the assassination of President Lincoln, Clay was torn between grief and rage. As he acknowledged the many sentiments of esteem and sadness flooding his legation desk, he pointed to Lincoln's "moderation in expression" and "firmness in action"—and to his own fervent hope that the president's martyrdom would "consecrate in the hearts of all men the principles of liberty and self-government." Though he admired the British for, of all people, "standing squarest in their shoes," he could not forget their official enmity during the rebellion. He presaged what history was to reveal: "England . . . carries too much sail for the bulk of her ship . . . the great Empire hastens to dissolution." He perceived that Lincoln's martyrdom lent strength to the liberal spirit of mankind everywhere, which would, in time, overthrow all autocracy.

By 1867 as the representative of a reunited country Clay had the opportunity to put some old wrongs into new perspective, and he did not hesitate to assert himself. Under the pretext of protecting European investments in Mexico, slippery Napoleon III had taken advantage of a convulsed America to send a French army into the country and forcibly establish Archduke Maximilian of Austria as his puppet-emperor, hoping that the Union would fall and leave the way open for French colonial ambitions. Now that hope was doomed. The French troops were withdrawn, a Mexican Republic was declared, and Maximilian fell before a firing squad. When, in the presence of Clay and members of other legations, an Austrian nobleman lamented the shooting of the archduke, the American minister struck with sarcasm: even more was it "to be regretted" that French troops "should have shot Mexicans wearing uniforms, and fighting in defense of their homes against a foreign invader; it is not, therefore, strange that when fortune favored them, those poor barbarians should have followed so illustrious an example." While the Russians present "much enjoyed" seeing Austria "cut to the very core," Clay knew the remark was "wormwood" to the Austrians.

The unsuccessful attempt to assassinate Czar Alexander II six months after the tragedy at Ford's Theater became another bond between the two nations. In a common animosity toward England's ambitions in the northern Pacific, the two emerging powers were brought together over the issue of Russian America—or Alaska. During the Crimean War in the 1850s, Russia had considered arranging a fictitious sale of the property to an American company in California, but the stratagem, it was believed, could be too easily detected and might provoke England into seizing the territory. In arranging for the Russian-American telegraph line, Cassius Clay as early as 1863 had "urged Russia to put the privileges" subleased until 1867 to the English Hudson Bay Company "into United States hands." Such a move, he reasoned, would render the natives of the region friendly in case of war with England. The American minister's influence with Alexander II had indicated the possibility of Russia's passing a "fee simple title" to lands in Alaska for necessary depots, or fortified outposts, for the owners of the American telegraph line.

Again, while the Russian fleet was in American waters during 1863–1864, Rear Admiral Popoff, in command of the squadron in the northern Pacific, had written Alexander's brother: "There are twenty million Americans, everyone of them a freeman. They have taken California and Oregon and sooner or later, they will get Alaska. It cannot be prevented and it would be better to yield with good grace and cede the territory to them. . . . Europeans [may] sneer at the Monroe Doctrine and Manifest Destiny, but if they were better acquainted with the Americans, they would know that these very ideas are in their blood and in the air they breathe."

Chancellor Gortchacow believed that ceding Alaska to the United States would be an effective blow against Great Britain. This was substantially the position that Czar Nicholas had taken nearly twenty years earlier, as Clay learned in 1863 from Robert J. Walker, who had been Polk's secretary of the treasury. Then Clay had impressed upon Walker the importance of owning the whole northwestern Pacific coast. Always an enthusiastic annexationist, Walker was later hired by Baron Edouard Stoeckl, the Russian minister in Washington, to aid in "facilitating" the Alaskan purchase. From the time of the Russian-American telegraph negotiations in 1863, Clay had ample opportunity to gain a "superior knowledge of the resources of Alaska"—its furs, timber, mineral potential, agricultural possibilities, and the immensely valuable fishing grounds extending from the Bering Sea to the Washington territory. He compiled this information and sent copies to Seward, congressmen, and interested "men of affairs on the West Coast, hoping to arouse them to an interest in the final purchase of the land."

Considering Russia's difficulty in administering the distant territory, its long-festering fear that Great Britain would seize the territory, the many common interests of the United States and Russia, the desire of both to keep the British out of northern Pacific waters, the two nations' manifestations of friendship in recent crises, and Clay's efforts to strengthen this friendship, the transfer of the area seems, in retrospect, to have been inevitable.

Desirous of protecting and expanding West Coast commercial interests, Senator Cornelius Cole of California made an effort in 1866 to secure the Alaskan rights of the British Hudson Bay Company, due for renewal by the Russian government in 1867, for the newly formed California Fur Company. Baron Stoeckl immediately informed Clay, upon the advice of Seward. In February 1867, Clay wrote Seward that a decision must be made by

June, for then the lease expired and the British company desired a twenty-five-year renewal. The matter was urgent. It remained for Seward and his aides to arrange the details of the purchase, which followed in March, thus cutting the British out of Alaska.

Senator Sumner in a speech to the Senate hailed the acquisition as a "new expression of that *Entente Cordiale* between the two powers which is a phenomenon of history." Even though the statement came from a political enemy, no higher praise could have been paid the American minister in Russia. Clay later wrote Seward that it was "owing to the good relations which I have been able to maintain with Russia that such a purchase was possible," while in the same letter he took Congress to task for their injustice and ingratitude in delaying payment to Russia for more than a year. Near the end of his life Clay summarized some of these points in a controversial speech at Berea College in which he stated that he wanted only one word with his name on his tombstone: "ALASKA."

Although Mary Jane had made a favorable impression in the Saint Petersburg court and was socially at home in Russia, as the Baltic winter wore on she became discontent. With their son Brutus and four daughters, one of whom was too delicate to endure the rigorous weather, she made plans to return to the Bluegrass. Clay wrote his brother Brutus in January 1862 that Mary Jane would be leaving the following month, and he later complained that she left "contrary to my wishes, and regardless of my protest."

When Clay was reappointed in 1863, his wife refused to accompany him on his return to Russia or to follow him later. Even so, he left Mary Jane his power of attorney to manage the large estate, with his brother's help and advice. The rental value of the property alone during the remaining years of his ministry he estimated at about $80,000. In addition to his salary, he acknowledged, he made a small fortune during these years speculating in

Missouri and United States stocks. With Mary Jane's diligent management at home and his success abroad, Clay soon paid off all his debts, which at one time had totaled as much as $60,000. During this same period the magnificent reconstruction of White Hall was completed, at a cost of about $30,000. Mary Jane was also busy encouraging and guiding the education and social development of her children, who were maturing into young adults.

Clay advised his children by mail on subjects as various as their reading, educational plans, and religious affiliations. He was especially proud of Laura's fluent French, and in 1866 he sent the seventeen-year-old a bracelet. Earlier he had obtained an interest in the oil wells of southern Russia for his eldest soldier son, Green; but although the wells were later worth millions, the venture failed. As the volunteer aide of General William Nelson at the Battle of Richmond, in August 1862, Green had borne his wounded superior off the field and taken him through the Confederate lines to safety in Jessamine County. Green's health failed during the war and he turned to farming, with the help of a mortgage loan from his mother. He was now married.

But at the other side of the earth, Clay was lonely. He frequented the fashionable clubs of the capital, was considered a desirable and colorful guest, and entertained distinguished groups at his own fine lodgings not far from the storied *Bronze Horseman* of Falconet, "the Peter monument" in Clay's phrase. For a time he was the favorite of the Empress Marie, whom he attracted first by speaking to her in public without first being spoken to—a breach of etiquette which was the talk of foreign legations. The empress was sympathetic, however, and found pleasure in their conversations; she made a point of renewing their talks in public. Clay saw her as "a woman of good sense, and great sweetness of disposition and features." In his opinion she was "a most lovely woman, mentally and morally," but her feelings were mixed about the responsibilities of leadership, a topic of conversation between them. They exchanged photographs of each other and their families.

The emperor, too, was pleased with Clay's society and conferred upon him the use of his elegant carriage. Another of Clay's friends—and he remarked that he often preferred the society of women to that of men—was the Princess Louise Suwarrow, a famous beauty, whom he remembered for her liveliness, her "very large and languishing blue eyes," and her luxuriantly long hair, which reminded him of the women of Toluca. As Clay was riding in the imperial carriage along the lake of the royal resort area of Tsarskoe Seló, he saw the princess with her servant rowing on the lake. Clay had the carriage drawn up and at her invitation took a seat with her in the boat. A sudden rain squall blew out of the North. As the lady was lightly dressed, Clay offered her the carriage, which conveyed her and her servant to her home while he waited under the trees for its return.

Clay thought he had done what any gentleman would under the circumstances, but allowing any other woman to be seen in the emperor's carriage was a gaucherie for which the empress never fully forgave him. He soon learned that his gallantry had created a scandal, which he later believed was used against him politically in the United States.

Many of the attacks made upon Clay while he was at Saint Petersburg may well have been the result of personal as well as political jealousies. An uncommonly handsome man in the prime of life, charming and personable, virile and outgoing, he naturally attracted women to him, even as he was attracted to them. One night in a grove at Krásnoe Seló, while thousands of hanging lamps illuminated the dance platform, hundreds of couples danced an old-fashioned cotillion, "swinging corners" in animated pleasure. Clay was standing by the emperor when the beautiful Princess Dolgorouki, who was dancing, turned to swing and lost her partner. Clay, who knew the princess well, immediately stepped into the dance and turned her, then stepped back again to the emperor's side.

"Were you dancing?" the emperor asked, surprised.

"No," Clay replied, "but the young lady seemed to be bewildered, and I came to her relief."

The emperor smiled with delight at Clay's gallantry.

Later, the same Princess Dolgorouki, who was one of Empress Marie's "dames d'honneur," invited Clay to her apartment in the Winter Palace near the Hermitage. He accepted, but later, as he was conducted by an elaborately adorned avant-courier with immense ostrich feathers in his headdress through what seemed acres of apartments, all along the way taking the salutes of guards who presented arms and cracked their muskets to the floor, he began to reflect upon the wisdom of his acceptance. "Might it not be a woman's freak?" he wondered, in some apprehension. At length he arrived at the princess's rooms. "It was certainly a relief to me," he wrote, "that I was not alone . . . with a charming woman!" It was, after all, an innocent Sunday levee. "But," Clay swore, "I never paid any more visits to the maids of honor."

Nevertheless, gossip persisted that they may well have visited him. It was rumored that the American minister was besieged with Russian women, who found him so attractive that some of them sought to bring their trunks to his rooms on Golanaia Street. In that great capital of a thousand intrigues, Clay probably did not always observe the proprieties. The only time he mentions the duello in his *Memoirs* in relation to Russia is to say that it is "forbidden by law . . . yet fights take place in private." In that situation, "if the parties are only wounded, they are supposed to have taken a tour abroad," but "if . . . one or more . . . are killed, then concealment is not possible." Stories persist that Clay fought several duels "in private," although such reports are doubtless exaggerated. The accounts, at any rate, are sparse, often vague, and generally speculative. They contend that he found himself challenged to duels by Russian noblemen, but that their expectations of victory over the Kentucky barbarian were frustrated by his skill with the bowie knife. Bellicose duelists were said to be outraged with the American's domination of them. A story of the day records that two such men sought Clay out in order to insult him first—and thus cleverly provoke a challenge. Then, according to the code, *they* could select the weapons—swords or pistols—and so evade the dreaded knife.

The two of them found the tall Kentuckian dining one evening in a fashionable restaurant. One of them ceremonially unrolled his gloves, then stepped up and cracked Clay across the face with them. In less than an eyeblink Clay threw a macelike fist into the nose and mouth of the would-be *duelliste*. The surprise blow was delivered with such force that the man's body broke completely through a nearby table, leaving a swath of food and shattered china for several yards. Clay glared at the victim's companion until he, too, shrank away, dragging his hapless friend with him. The minister said not a word but sat down at his table and continued his meal.

Clay was considered, if not always a man of the world with his strange western ways and flawed French, *un homme que cet homme-là*—a true man, every inch of him. He was also thought to be *"démocratique,"* a breath of fresh air in a rigid society, a man who broke through all etiquette so far as to be affable to all classes alike. But at his own lavish parties and balls he outdid the Russian aristocracy. His orchestras were larger and better than theirs, and there was always a special touch—his remarkable Bluegrass punch, for example. The women, especially, preferred this to the usual champagne and frequently tried to secure the recipe. He pleased the cream of Saint Petersburg society at the mansion of Princess Kotzoubey on the Nevsky Prospekt, where members of the royal family, sometimes even the Empress Marie herself, could be seen. But he visited the freedmen of the countryside too and in their modest cottages or on rustic tables under trees enjoyed *shchi* and *chernyi khleb*, or cabbage soup and black rye bread. Often he participated in the Russian ceremony of hospitality, the *khleb-sol'*, or the taking of bread and salt with the family.

He frequented the new Maryinsky Theatre, named in honor of the empress. Over the years, he became a ballet enthusiast like his good friend Chancellor Gortchacow, and Kentucky legend persists that, among his several adventures in Russia and Europe, his deepest *affaire de coeur* was with a member of the Imperial Ballet. Her name is obscured in time and secrecy, inventive interpretations and embellished conjecture. For decades, though, she has most frequently been called Anna Petroff. Her loveliness, dark-eyed and nymphlike, is obvious to anyone who goes to White Hall and sees the portrait—supposed by many to be hers—hanging in the grand ballroom.* Of all the *premières danseuses,* she was the only one Clay remembered with such tender sentiments.

Of their meeting, we know next to nothing. Perhaps he saw her first in some divertissement, or at the Maryinsky's *foyer de la danse,* where it was the custom for balletomanes to gather—government officials, distinguished guests, nobles, generals, and wealthy sponsors. There he could have seen her and other dancers doing their exercises "on the *barre*" before massive pier glass mirrors. Clay described the ballet as "a mimic melo-drama," a plot "intermingled with dances and poses, as easily understood as words. Nothing lascivious in the least is ever allowed; and, with postures which would make an American woman blush to the very hair, a ballet-girl will wear

* Concerning the White Hall portrait, my own research, at the present time at least, points to the possibility that its subject is Marie Sergeevna Surovschikova Petipa, the famed ballerina of the magnificent flowering of classic Russian ballet in the third quarter of the nineteenth century. For further details, see "Addendum: The Russian Ballerina."

the face of innocence and unconsciousness which might be called angelic."

Clay noted in his *Memoirs* that in the society of Saint Petersburg *"liaisons* are very common," and "it is not thought discreditable to have a mistress." Even in the home of Prince Gortchacow a beautiful woman lived, who in Saint Petersburg passed as his niece. In court circles, then, it is possible that the relationship of Clay and his ballerina went unquestioned. Perhaps in the winters they shot down the artificially constructed ice mountains in sleds at terrific speeds, or in parties of courtiers bundled together under fur lap robes in troikas and swept the icy corners, as they set out to dances held beneath the smoke-stained masterpieces in the Hermitage. There Catherine the Great had ordered the inscription placed at the entrance: "Leave all ranks outside together with hats and especially swords."

Upon the frozen Neva, they gathered with merry groups in large colorful tents and skated upon the artificially smoothed ice. One evening Clay and his ballerina, so the legend goes, joined members of the imperial family in torchlight, and with three other couples led the dancers upon the ice in the majestic quadrille. Afterward, perhaps, they skated off to the royal tent to warm themselves on blanketed stoves, take food from the sumptuous *zakuska* tables, and drink vodka flavored with lemon peel and cherry stones.

As enchanted as the winter evenings must have been, the white summer nights of Saint Petersburg were, as Clay later recalled, "the wonder of all who have been so fortunate as to witness them." He described them as "an extended twilight, where print can be read all the time by the light of the stars and the refracted rays of the sun ill-concealed beneath the near horizon." We assume he shared the light of such nights with his ballerina in his beach house by the Neva. Together they watched the boats filled with lovers, as he later wrote of them, "given to poetry and romance—where words of love are breathed in softened tones into willing ears. . . . weird strains of the music died away in the distant theater. . . . It seemed . . . that we were borne by some magic power into the intensified poetry and beauty of a Russian summer night."

For Clay, we speculate, it could hardly have been otherwise, for he was not only a formidable diplomat, but also a true romantic.

9

ULYSSES AT ITHACA

W HEN HE CAME HOME after the Trojan War and his long wanderings, Ulysses did not recognize his own country. His rage when he saw the state of things in Ithaca was hardly greater than that of Cassius Marcellus Clay upon his return to America in the fall of 1869. Unlike Ulysses, however, Clay was not set ashore unconscious of recent events at home. He had long been apprehensive of the bitter fruit the Civil War was to bear. Early in the conflict Clay had gone to the secretary of war to intervene on behalf of a southerner, "taken in New York by Stanton's secret police," so Clay said, "and brought to Washington a prisoner." In an "insolent tone," Stanton snapped at him: "It is a pretty state of affairs when men of your position, with the commission of a Foreign Minister in your pocket, should be found interceding for the liberation of traitors."

Clay replied, "I will let you know that I am your equal and care no more for your opinions than those of any other citizen. There are ten millions of men in rebellion. Do you expect to execute them all? Or, rather, is not the war to be put down by judicious clemency, as well as force?" And so saying, Clay took up his hat and left.

In time, the two men reconciled their differences. Stanton wrote Clay in a tone of relief: "For your . . . support I am thankful. . . . Of my failings and short-comings I am conscious, and deeply regret them when they give offense to friends whose regard I esteem." This was "manly," Clay thought. It was not the first time that members of the early radical contingent of antislavery men would differ among themselves, nor the only time they would resolve their differences.

As far as Clay was concerned, Reconstruction began in 1862 when Lincoln issued the Emancipation Proclamation. Aware of approaching problems before he returned to Russia in the spring of 1863, he wrote, "Now, for the first time, it began to be discussed—as the tide of battle, after the Proclamation, turned in our favor—what shall be done with the conquered States?" If he had been extreme in his view of how the war should be conducted, he was moderate in his view of reunion. With some qualifications, he shared with Lincoln during the early years of the rebellion the old legal theory of the impossibility of secession. Cutting through the whole "pernicious abstraction" of whether the rebel states were, all through the war, still in the Union, Clay later urged essentially what Lincoln elaborated two nights before his assassination—"the necessity," once the rebellion was put down, of again getting "the seceded states, so called . . . into proper practical relation" to the Union. Like his old antislavery co-workers, he favored the ballot for the blacks, but unlike many Republicans he would have no part of a federally imposed social revolution. In his opinion such a course would only alienate the southern states from Republicanism and, in the long run, embitter the old sectional strife.

By 1866, the time of the break between Andrew Johnson and Congress on this very question, Clay believed himself alienated from Seward and what he termed the secretary's "pro-slavery policy." Perhaps he was referring to what he had considered Seward's too-eager readiness to compromise the slavery issue for prospects of political success, evident as early as their Washington meeting in 1860. But he may have had in mind Seward's plan for a postwar coalition of moderate Republicans and Democrats that would defeat the policies of both radical Republicans and peace Democrats.

Clay's view was that the former Whigs of the border states and the South should provide the leadership of a strong Unionist movement, bringing the new freedmen with them into Republican ranks. The policy was not impractical—at least during the early post–Civil War period. In Mississippi, for example, old-line Whigs often worked with Negroes, sometimes effectively, in the frequently misrepresented role of "scalawag"; they did so in preference to joining the Democratic party. "Men who think that 'the war' knocked all the Old Whig spirit out of the Whigs," one of them declared, "are just . . . fatally mistaken." Remembering that Constitutional Unionist John Bell in the election of 1860 had carried Kentucky and most of the other border states, as well as his native Tennessee, Clay was understandably concerned that Republican hopes in the South would be endangered by a Seward compromise with the Democrats. Radical Republicans such as Salmon P. Chase agreed. But Clay, on the other hand, also feared that if extreme measures were pushed in the South by the radicals, the newly won contingent of Republican voters would be driven into a resurgent Democratic party. In the process, the new freedmen might well be abandoned to the tender mercies of the old proslavery elements.

Clay accurately perceived that the impeachment proceedings against Johnson would set back the Republican party and its hopes for future success. Writing from Saint Petersburg, March 13, 1866, Clay denounced "the course of Sumner and Stevens," contending, "Let the States give freedmen all civil rights, and by degrees extend to them the right of suffrage," but asserting this important qualification: "Or else let an amendment of the Constitution make one rule of suffrage for all the States." Anticipating the Fifteenth Amendment of 1870, Clay was convinced from the outset of Reconstruction that Unionist elements of the border and southern states could be held to Republicanism and strengthened if they were not driven away by unfair treatment.

Grant soon proved that he was no Lincoln in his ability to bring together radical and conservative interests in government. It was a time of rampant corruption, and most of it was not of Grant's making—the Boss Tweed outrages, the Gould-Fisk effort to corner the gold market, the Erie stock manipulation. But Grant had been a guest on one of Fisk's steamboats. He was insensitive enough in his social relationships to hobnob with John McDonald, the notorious leader of the Whiskey Ring, and make him first his political boss in Missouri, later his supervisor of internal revenue. He protected his private secretary, Orville E. Babcock, of whom Grant's biographer William, B. Hesseltine noted that he "fished for gold in every stinking cesspool." Grant seemed blind to the quality of his governmental appointments; his rank nepotism confounded honest men of all parties and alienated many Radical Republicans. Shortly before Clay returned from Russia, his old antislavery friend, Indianian George W. Julian, noted in his diary that Republicanism was in trouble and a reorganization of parties was inevitable.

Clay came out of his Baltic lair like a lion. The exploited people of Cuba had risen in rebellion against Spain in 1868, and he lost no time in assailing the Grant administration for allowing Spanish gunboats to be equipped in New York harbor while Cuban ships were confiscated. It has been the historical policy of the democracy, he pointed out, to aid "revolutionary people of the American Continent . . . against their autocratic masters in Europe." He organized the Cuban Charitable Aid Society and rallied Horace Greeley, Charles A. Dana, and such regionally strong Republicans as Senator Benjamin F. Wade of Ohio to the cause. Obvious political efforts were made to silence Clay when he spoke at the Cooper Institute in New York, but the crudity of such moves exposed their perpetrators. In fiery epithet as of old, Clay lashed out at the "greedy cormorants, political *laz*[*z*]*aroni*, and treasury-robbers of a sick Party."

Clay became a pioneer in the Liberal Republican movement, joining Sumner, Greeley, Chase, Julian, Trumbull, and other opponents of the Grant administration. Attempting to pull even the radical Henry Wilson into the fold, he posed the question: "Is it too late to save the fruits of the war by a generous course—an honest capable man at the head of affairs?" He corresponded with Frederick Douglass, publisher of the *North Star*. Attacking Grant, he explained his position with characteristic force and candor:

Whilst it would have been good policy as I think to have executed a few leading rebels promptly—it certainly is bad policy to keep up proscription and irritation after all prospects of [an] *oppressive* policy [are] past. In this [Massachusetts] Governor [John A.] Andrew—one of the truest and wisest of our friends—agreed with me. I have no fear with you that the fruits of the war are to be lost by a *liberal policy* towards the South. On the contrary the danger to the Blacks is in . . . widening . . . the difference between the Whites and Blacks—the whites being superior in number and at present in intelligence & wealth in the South. . . . All experience shows that no party can live long in a free country—and I would wish the Blacks to show magnanimity to the rebels—that they might in turn in the day of need receive it.

On July 4, 1871, Clay delivered a widely publicized oration to an immense crowd of both blacks and whites in Lexington. A newspaper account reported that he advocated " 'impartial suffrage,' 'universal amnesty,' and a presidential candidate 'who came with the olive branch rather than the sword'—Horace Greeley."

In some ways the reformist Liberal Republicans had taken the pulse of the country. Their move against the corruption associated with the Grant administration, their advocacy of tariff reform, their reluctant willingness to work with Democrats on the basis of principle, if not of party (Horace White, editor of the influential *Chicago Tribune*, considered them "ex-Democrats"), initiated new attitudes toward both Republicans and Democrats and helped them to shake off the vestiges of the past. More specifically, their platform emphasized "local self-government," through which, they believed, the rights of all citizens could be secured more fully than through "any centralized power." They attacked the Enforcement Acts, asserting the dominance of the civil over military authority, and "freedom of person under the protection of . . . habeas corpus."

Yet most recent historians regard the Liberal Republicans as illiberal indeed, particularly in their southern policy. In advocating home rule, or self-government in local matters, they were playing into the hands of the Democrats and endangering the crusade for Negro rights.

In 1872, aided by his old college friend and best man, Missourian James S. Rollins, Clay engineered the successful nomination of Greeley, defeating all efforts to place Charles Francis Adams on the Liberal Republican ticket. At the convention in Cincinnati, Clay encountered "a small, flaxen-haired, chipper man," who asked him, of all things, to swing the Kentucky vote for Adams. For one of the few times in his life, Clay was nonplussed. This was, he said, the first time he had met the "brilliant, eccentric, and combustible" Henry Watterson of the *Louisville Courier-Journal*. Although he disliked the editor's support of Sewardite Adams, his "toadyism to the Grant men," and some of his other political views, he regretted making an enemy of the man who, in his judgment, was "the most potent politician in all the South."

Clay spoke widely in support of the reformist ticket and its principles. From New York and Ohio to Missouri and Kentucky he urged amnesty for southerners, civil service reform, and "purification" of the Grantites. Citizens had felt the boom—the cheery optimism and get-rich-quick clamor of what Mark Twain would call "The Gilded Age"; but schemes of private greed, exploitation of the country's resources, and the unholy wedding of business and politics were to have their consequences. The Panic of 1873 and its subsequent depression lay around the corner. Growing charges of corruption distressed decent citizens all over the country. Many rallied under the slogan "Turn the rascals out!" But although he was a fierce moral force, Greeley proved an unlikely politician, and Clay was not surprised when he was beaten. The Grant administration had been proved vulnerable to attack, however, and the groundwork for the 1876 election was laid.

Clay later was to write, "Those who follow principles can not always remain in the same party." To some it was a superb irony that the same man who had attacked and helped destroy Whiggery in the 1850s would now, in the 1870s, apply his verbal lash to radical Republicanism, but there was an inner consistency in his actions. His present plans—though rank apostasy in the view of radicals, echoing what they termed the "soft" policies of Lincoln and Johnson—Clay regarded as absolutely necessary to "the safety of the Republic." Rightly or wrongly, Clay believed in good faith that Republican principles had been perverted in the Grant administration. He later admitted that Grant may have been blind to the efforts of the politicians around him "to establish Caesarism in this Republic," as Clay put it, "by electing him to a third term." But the retrospect of history is tolerant, while to Clay the threat was very real. To elect Grant, he believed, would be "to strengthen the hands of the plunderers, and those engaged in the overthrow of State autonomy."

So Cassius Clay deliberately set out to destroy a Republicanism he no longer recognized. To that end he joined the Democratic party in 1875, explaining that the issue was now "one of the most important that ever interested the human race . . . whether man is capable of self-government." The parties had changed, Clay was convinced, rather than his own view of things. Republican or Democrat, he was still a freedom hunter.

Before the convention, he was invited to canvass Mississippi. Clay's account of his experience there reminds one of what used to be called "Black Reconstruction"—a picture drastically modified by recent historians of the period. But if one takes Clay at his word, there must have been some realities behind the caricatures. In Greenville, where "the carpet-baggers, up to this time, had their own way," and "the outrages of misrule reached their highest culmination," radical appointees kept up the "bitterest feeling . . . between the whites and blacks for party purposes." Corrupt hirelings stuffed their pockets with loot, and the old planters got labor only with difficulty, paying "officials" for the privilege. Livestock was stolen, legal redress was nonexistent, and heavy taxes on cotton absorbed the profits. In short, general chaos reigned. Public monies, including the school fund at Jackson, were "plundered." Conditions became so intolerable, Clay observed, that the old planters were "abandoning the best cottonlands in the world." Even the most fortunate of the blacks themselves, clergymen and small landholders, fought oppressive taxation and other injustices.

Clay spoke to large audiences, mostly black, in Mississippi. He exposed "liars" and called them so to their faces, producing evidences of fraud. "I never felt in more danger in my life," he said, "not that they would care to kill me particularly, but because in a *melée* they would not care who was killed." He singled out radicals who had embroiled blacks and whites at Vicksburg and Friar's Point. "Now I ask who was killed? If any men of the Radical party will tell me of one carpetbagger who was ever killed in these battles I will come down from this platform, be forever silent, and vote the Radical ticket."

"That's true!" someone in the crowd shouted. "They bring on the fight, and then run away!"

As a Democrat, Cassius Clay helped overthrow the radical Republican regime of Adelbert Ames in Mississippi by a 35,000-vote majority. In the judgment of some historians, the Ames administration was one of the best-intentioned and most estimable of the Reconstruction governments. Yet it was riddled with what Ames himself called "an audacious, pushing crowd" of northern carpet-baggers and fraudulent hirelings. In driving them out, the famed emancipationist who had been a hero of the North became a hero of the South.

On a more practical level, Clay had demonstrated his vote-getting ability in the South. Four years earlier, his leadership in the Liberal Republican movement, and his sagacity in drawing the Democrats into an independent alliance against the Grant Republicans had produced a victory for Greeley in most of the border states, including Kentucky. So as a liberal southerner, by 1875, he was given a chance of receiving the vice-presidential nomination for the second time in his life—and, singularly, in both major parties.

But it was not to be. Clay's fierce individualism, the storm cloud of violence that hovered over him all his life, the calumnies of his enemies, and what the public considered intolerable personal eccentricities all militated against his candidacy in 1876. As he had been trapped between the abolitionist cranks of the North and the fanatic slavery interests of the South, he was now the object of the hatred and ridicule of the Grant Republicans of the North and, because of his long and colorful record as a Republican emancipationist, not fully acceptable to the old-line Democrats of the South. Thus, when Samuel J. Tilden, who had successfully prosecuted "Boss" Tweed, received the presidential nomination, it was not the Kentuckian Clay, but instead the Indianian Thomas A. Hendricks who garnered the necessary delegate support for second place on the national Democratic ticket.

Yet a high cabinet post was virtually assured him, should he prefer it to retirement. So he campaigned forcefully from Mississippi to Ohio. After the votes were in, he was made president of the convention held in Louisville during the controversy that followed Tilden's apparent election. In Clay's words, "Samuel J. Tilden was triumphantly elected President of the United States. It was no fault of mine that he was, by Democratic treachery and cowardice, and Republican fraud and bull-dozing, not allowed to take the place to which the people, by a majority of her electoral and popular vote, had assigned him." After an elaborate compromise, President Rutherford B. Hayes withdrew the Federal troops occu-pying the last of the "unredeemed" states—South Caro-lina and Louisiana. With that gesture, in the eyes of many of his countrymen, Hayes closed the volume of Recon-struction in American history.

Clay now could return to White Hall in peace, and, as he sighed in his *Memoirs*, "be allowed to hang my arms upon the wall"—or so it seemed. Here then, as he ap-proached his seventies, the "two great acts in the Political Drama," in which he had borne "a soldier's part," were to be concluded: "The first was the freedom of the blacks, and the equality of all before the law. The second was the restoration of the States to their original sovereignty. The Union is restored. There is a Nation. I trust it will remain forever one and indivisible— the sacred ark of the liber-ties of all our people, and the beacon light of progress for all nations of the earth."

Mary Jane Clay had worked hard during the years her husband was gone from White Hall—managing the huge estate from planting time to harvest, keeping the ac-counts, seeing to the children's educations, and helping some of them to get settled into their marriages. Four had died. Six had lived into maturity: Green (who would die in 1883), Brutus, Mary Barr, Sarah (Sallie), Laura, and Anne. She had also watched the new mansion rise brick by brick. Given the moral standards of her time and place, Mary Jane Clay had reason for indignation. She had more than a faint idea of those luring sirens, the Saint Petersburg princesses and youth-endowing Calypsos of the Maryinsky Theatre. After all, she remembered some of them—and had heard about others. And what she did not know, her garrulous sister Anne was determined she *should* know.

Cool and aloof, she had written Clay before he left New York in 1870, indicating in a businesslike way her desire to purchase the cemetery lot in Lexington where four of their children were buried. The implication was clear enough, for he owned a plot in the Richmond Cemetery where his remains were to be interred. If Mary Jane desired separation from him in death, as her letter indicated, then she probably already considered herself separated from him in life.

Upon his return to White Hall, Mary Jane first put Cassius into a separate room of the new house. Then, when the weather turned cold, without consulting him, she moved all his clothes into another room where the fireplace was unfinished. "The cold was so intense," he later wrote, "that icicles froze on my beard." But he flattered himself that it was his own fault if he did not go into her room, where a fire was always kept blazing.

One night, however, she sent for him to come to her room to look over and settle their business accounts. This he did, and seeing them in his favor, as he showed her, Mary Jane proposed to pay him what she owed him. "This," he claimed, "my instincts as a husband and gentleman forbade me to accept; for, perhaps, unhappily for me, a love of money was not one of my vices."

Then, according to Clay, Mary Jane lost her temper. Infuriated, she let loose a catalog of his "faults and escapades of a lifetime." She "poured them upon my devoted head like a deluge." He was stunned into silence, for in nearly forty years of married life, despite their differences, "angry words had never been heard." At first, he said, "I was indignant," and ready to retort in kind, "for, after I had married her, my love for her was pure and devoted, *and it was she who made the first breach upon the marriage duties."*

But as she went on, Clay alleged, "I grew calm; for now the last touch of love had vanished," and he let her continue. "I finally, with suave tones, bade her good-night, and returned to my room, and locked the door after me ever afterward during her stay in my house."

What had begun as an impulsive marriage of passion had long since given way to innumerable differences, long absences from each other, and, during many of their married years, a financial strain which resulted in a kind of intrafamily property war. Clay, always proudhearted, never got over his bitterness at Mary Jane's refusal to return with him to Russia in 1863. Most of all, he could never forgive her for siding in moments of crisis with "my inveterate enemies, the Warfield clan," rather than with him. And with the exception of Green, Clay complained, his children knew little of him, receiving most of their ideas about him from the Warfields.

Mary Jane moved to Lexington for a time in the early 1870s to live with her sister Anne, returning to White Hall when convenient. On one occasion, at least, she attempt-ed a reconciliation. However, upon hearing of her com-ing, Clay stubbornly went to Green's house nearby. She sent a message by Green, saying that she *"loved me as much as she ever did."* But Clay refused to see her, and she returned to Lexington.

Philosophically, he turned to his books. He reread the classics and mulled over his favorites from Homer and Shakespeare to Pope and Byron. In daylight hours, he sought companionship in nature, luring the redbirds to his crumb box by the library window.

But at night he was more lonely than ever. By the piazza, he sat out under the moon and stars, speculating upon his life, baffled "like Manfred," and "calling for sympathy with the mute worlds in vain!" He solilo-quized, "Had I been worse than other men?" Was his exile the punishment of violated laws? "I, who had sacrificed all to men, was by men left to myself alone." It was his habit in such moments of self-torture to go up to his bedroom and throw open the shutters. The whirring bats entered, their wings beating the starlight, and picked the flies from the white plaster walls: "their fluttering—life—life—was a great pleasure to me."

His loneliness shook loose the memory of another time, another place, and Clay buried his sadness in recollection of "that one voice which for so many years in a strange land I had listened to as the sweetest music." She materialized in his dreams: "I saw the imploring looks, and heard the calling for me of the lost one."

In the great city of infinite intrigues, Saint Petersburg, there was born in 1866 a male child. "To the secret of his parentage," he stated decades later, "I am the only living witness—I who have, of all men living, the best reason to know—and that secret will die with me." In the early 1870s, Clay brought his "adopted child," Leonide Petroff, from Russia, assumed guardianship from the boy's "nominal parents," and had his name changed to "Launey Clay" and entered in Madison County court records.

If fact is consistent with local legend, at the time of the boy's arrival Cassius and Mary Jane Clay still shared a kind of marriage of convenience. From time to time, she came to White Hall, where they apparently lived in separate rooms, and as his political obligations required, they entertained lavishly on these occasions.

During one of these evenings of entertainment, when the windows of the mansion were ablaze with candlelight and the grand ballroom overflowing with Bluegrass society, a coach drove up from the direction of Lexington. Clay excused himself from a group of men at the corner of the house, strode through wreathed cigar smoke, and made his way down to the carriage. There he received one or two women—accounts vary—each veiled and in dark dress, and a small boy about four years old. "General Clay," one of the women said distinctly, "I have brought you your son from Russia."

He bowed in his courtly fashion. "May I take him up into the light and look at him?"

Acquiescing, the women waited, while Clay took the child's hand and led him up to the front entrance of White Hall and into the brilliant light of the chandelier. He introduced the child as "my adopted son from Russia," then returned him to the care of the veiled women, spoke a few words with them, and helped them back into the carriage. They drove off in the direction of Richmond, and the general came back up to join his guests.

But the party broke up soon afterward. One can imagine how little peace Anne and the other Warfields gave Mary Jane after this incident. She moved permanently to Lexington and purchased a house there. Although all of his children except Green opposed the divorce action Cassius brought, Mary Jane let the case go without resistance, and the decree was granted February 7, 1878, on the grounds of abandonment. Of course, the conservative community of Richmond was shocked. "Some women of Richmond of doubtful reputation," Clay observed, "tried to drive Launey and myself from society"; and his own daughters were equally disapproving. An editor of the *Cincinnati Enquirer* exploded in a heat of self-righteous outrage: "You see an early champion of freedom walking about boastfully with a bastard son, imported like an Arabian cross of horses, and swearing at his family."

Cassius Clay, we gather, had expected no less from public or family. It was not the first time he had accepted the role of outcast and eccentric.

"As, after the mob at Lexington," he said, "I walked down the streets with calm indifference to my persecutors, so here, having made up my mind as to my highest duty, I calmly shouldered all the responsibility of my action." In the years following that memorable night at White Hall, the old general could be seen riding about the countryside with his son behind him—or at his side on a horse of his own. He made a financial arrangement with Green which provided Launey with a sixth interest in his White Hall estate, as the other children had.

His homecoming had been an unquiet return. Like Ulysses, Clay had roamed far with a hungry heart. But in the midst of a still active political career, he recognized a duty nearer at hand. He had seen to it. Now, with his mythic counterpart, he could look upon his blood and say, "This is my son, mine own Telemachus."

10

TWILIGHT AT WHITE HALL

IN 1845, WHILE HE was deeply embroiled in antislavery activities, Clay had been firmly convinced that two of his infant children were poisoned by their Negro nurse, Emily. Since slaves who had grievances against their masters had little chance for redress in the courts of law, such crimes sometimes occurred as acts of revenge. In the death of one of the children, his namesake Cassius, the charge was poisoning by arsenic in milk. Clay always believed that the jury that acquitted the nurse was "bulldozed" by his political enemies, and that Emily and her relatives had all along been part of a conspiracy to hurt him by taking the lives of his helpless children. Decades later, when he began to notice that his adopted son, Launey, was not thriving, but gradually losing his vivacity and growing increasingly listless, the aging man's suspicions were aroused.

At this time, he and Launey were living alone in White Hall. He had only black employees, the house servants including Sarah and David White and a nurse for Launey. The Whites had a son named Perry, who frequently visited his parents and, apparently, Launey's nurse. Although Sarah had often urged Clay to hire Perry, Clay considered him a "general loafer." He did nothing productive, and yet he rode a fine horse and sat a fine saddle. He dressed well, always went armed, and practiced his pistol shots at trees in the White Hall pastures—until Clay forbade it.

"Of all men," he later wrote, "I am the least suspicious when my confidence is once gained." Old as he was, Clay was not blind, and although he might wink at petty thievery, being plundered was another matter. He observed that many of his house supplies were disappearing, the duplicate keys of his safe were taken, and, at length, the silver was missing from the safe. Then he noticed that Launey began to drop objects from his "half-paralyzed hands," and to vomit frequently. Clay tasted the child's food. The milk, especially, had a peculiar flavor, or so he thought, reason struggling with emotion. Perhaps the taste could be attributed to the wild herbage where the cattle grazed, but he was edgy with worry.

Finally Clay intercepted a letter from Perry White, threatening his life. The young black's motivation apparently was a wish to take Launey's nurse immediately from White Hall and marry her. Perry White was quoted as saying that he "was as good as old Cash Clay, or any other white man, and if he [Clay] fooled with him . . . he would kill him." In another letter, he reportedly wrote that he "did not care for Cash Clay, and if he ever got a chance, he intended to kill him," and he so publicly boasted.

"Then I saw all," Clay concluded. Nearly seventy now, the old general was at first paralyzed with despair. He could expect little help from county officials, who opposed his politics. He had no confidence in their efficiency. Then, in his own words, "The philanthropy of a life-time melted as the dew before a summer's sun." He sternly resolved, "I will stand on the eternal laws of self-defense of me and mine."

Once his mind was made up, Clay asserted, "I never felt more calm in my life." He armed himself, often with a shotgun, always with a revolver and bowie knife. Keeping his own counsel, and having made a detailed list of his losses, he told Sarah and David White to leave in fifteen minutes, "if they desired to live." In less than five minutes the couple were on a run for Foxtown. Through the father, Clay sent warning to Perry White not to come on his land again. He also packed up the nurse and sent her off.

Shortly afterward, General Clay set out in search of new servants, taking Launey up on his mount with him, behind the saddle. As they approached the stable, the keen eyes of the old general discerned a movement in the woods. It was Perry White. Riding closer, Clay stopped, dismounted, and with pistol in hand advanced rapidly upon the man, confronting him and demanding that he hold up his hands. This White did, but as Clay questioned him, White suddenly sprang for his weapons and attempted to draw. Clay fired, striking him in the neck, then again through the heart.

Clay turned himself over to the authorities immediately but was exonerated. Apparently even his enemies accepted the "imperative necessity" of his action. As an editor of the *Saint Louis Republican* commented, "It was certainly a curious freak of fortune which compelled Cassius M. Clay, at the close of a long and prominent public career, to kill a member of a race which he championed so gallantly and persistently in early days."

In 1875 Clay's son Brutus, then twenty-eight years old and a graduate of the University of Michigan, decided to run for the House of Representatives in Madison County as a Republican. Clay had recently done much to build up the Democratic party and did not hesitate to speak to his Democratic friends, remind them of his service to the party, and seek their support for his son. His reasoning was that "there were but a few Republicans in the Legislature," and that "excessive majorities were not desirable in a Republic." His suggestions were met with "contempt and even indignation." Although Clay's personal life—his flouting of the local mores—was probably the focus of much of the hostility against him, the answer of the Madison County Democrats was more equivocal. Brutus had married a woman of fortune, Pattie A. Field, and, "if once in the ascendency," they asserted, "could not be easily ousted again."

Violence began to build, and rancor toward the Clays grew savage. On the evening before election, Green Clay and a Dr. Roberts, in company with a white voter, Adam Butner, were on their way home at dusk on the Stringtown turnpike when they were assaulted by about twenty men following them on horseback. The exchange of fire was so thick that Clay's and Roberts's clothes were perforated with bullet holes and Butner was shot dead on his horse. Clay and Roberts put spurs to their horses and escaped. When they reported the incident to Clay, he grimly advised Green, "Return to the same precinct next day, and defend the rights of [yourself] and [your] brother's friends to a free ballot, or die."

Meanwhile, opposing Democrats set up a camp in the Foxtown neighborhood. There they induced blacks to enter, provided them with music, food, and liquor, and kept them drinking and having a good time until they could be voted en masse against Brutus. Upon hearing this, Clay immediately moved against them. He also formed a camp, fed the voters, and defied "the Democratic Nihilists," as he dubbed them. "I sent word that we were 'ready for them.' " Clay declared, "The party was never before so much in arms."

He marched the blacks from his camp "in columns of twos, with all the arms I could obtain from them, and all I had, in my rockaway." He placed a guard over the carriageful of weapons about a hundred yards from the polls, which were held in the cattle-scales in warm weather. With the serene demeanor that had come to characterize his resolute conviction, he approached the polls. "I went alone and asked the judges to let my men vote." After consultation, they agreed, and the blacks, led by Clay's

Negro foreman, Tom Peyton, began to vote—sixty to eighty men in all.

As the voting commenced, the leader of the opposing Democrats stepped between Clay and the election officials and looked the old general sternly in the face. "We are ready for you," he said. This was the message Clay had earlier sent to the opposition. "I well understood what it meant," he reported. Clay later learned that large numbers of the "Democratic Nihilists," mostly whites, had stored shotguns and other weapons in anticipation of a battle. They were armed and waiting behind windows overlooking the polls. The few white Republicans of the Foxtown precinct were nowhere to be seen; they had been advised by the Democrats not to attend the election.

It was not so much Clay's keen intuition of danger that saved him as his common sense. Of course he was armed to the teeth, but so was the opposition. Now was the time for diplomacy, he sensed, not fighting. "My men were voting," he observed, "and a row would defeat my purpose; and so, with great self-command, I affected not to understand what was said, and made a pleasant reply." His equanimity in this situation proved more effective than his famed pugnacity, and further bloodshed at Foxtown was avoided.

At dusk Green Clay and a brave tenant, James O'Donnell, armed with shotguns and pistols, came to·the polls and voted. The vote was close. In the opinion of Clay and his friends, Brutus was elected by the legal votes but beaten illegally, especially in Richmond, by imported repeaters. As Clay had expected, no inquest was held over "the dead martyr, Adam Butner." No indictment was made by the grand jury. No publication of the injustice appeared in the Democratic papers. Only Clay lashed out in fiery rhetorical queries: "Was not the common law of the Solid South but carried out? Had not I and my family done that which the 'Solid South' has proclaimed to all the world shall not be done—'Organized the blacks'? And was not our crime [*sic*] death without redress in the courts?"

The proslavery forces had over the years managed to harass Clay severely, burning his barns and outbuildings, destroying stores of grain and an office building containing valuable papers. Although he had joined the Democratic fold in order to defeat the radical Republican policies in the South, once that purpose was achieved he returned to the old party he had never really left in principle. Some Democrats had frankly told him, "I will never vote for you, or your sons . . . because you took away from me my slaves, and I will never forgive you." By 1884, once more a self-declared Republican and campaigner for James G. Blaine, Clay spoke out in Louisville, equating the old ideas of the defenders of slavery with the new "Solid South," and vigorously attacking its despotism.

Even before he returned from Russia, he had believed that the Ku Klux Klan had declared its "vendetta" against him. Whether or not it had a hand in the Perry White altercation we shall probably never know; but the secret society did all it could to harass the old general. Signing its note "Ku Klux," the Klan declared its intention to kill Clay's freeborn Negro foreman, Tom Peyton, whom the society considered "obnoxious," probably because he was at the head of the black voters in the 1875 election that had created such a stir in the Bluegrass. Clay discussed it with his faithful employee and found him sensible and firm.

"Mars. Cash," he said, "I have done nothing to be killed for."

Looking at him, General Clay was reminded of the brave Chief Red Cloud. "What will you do: stand, or run for it?"

"If you will defend me, I will stand."

It was for Clay a very grave question. "I don't know that I shall be able to save you, or even myself; but, since you have the heart to defend yourself, I will stand by you to the death." Shortly after this incident, Clay began to refer to White Hall as a fort. Within the grounds of the mansion, aided by other faithful employees, the two proved invulnerable. But at the nearby Negro settlement of Needmore, Thomas Peyton was set upon and murdered by two blacks, one of whom held the foreman while the other stabbed him in the left side and back. The crime was committed in the presence of literally dozens of witnesses, both black and white; yet the perpetrators were cleared by the Madison County community. Clay believed that the murderers were "hired, or bulldozed, or both." That was the way of the Klan.

Clay's next two foremen, the Bowlin brothers, were also victims of masked violence. Klan members apparently killed the elder Bowlin, or hired a killer to do so. When the younger brother took his place as foreman, Clay advised him to arm and defend himself at all hazards. While riding one day, the young man found members of the Klan in close pursuit. Following the old general's advice, he turned and shot one of them dead. Bowlin was indicted and sentenced to the state penitentiary for life. As of old, Clay's pen jagged the paper in outrage: "If he deserves punishment, then do I, for I advised his course, and was the approver of it before and after the act, and am a *particeps criminis*."

Clay did not entirely drop from the public eye in the decade that followed. He stumped the country for Blaine in 1884. In his eighth presidential canvass in the North, he was delighted to support the man who had helped defeat Grant's "Caesarism" in 1880. For the two years following the Blaine campaign, Clay busied himself with his *Memoirs*, and published a 600-page volume in 1886. Although it received some favorable reviews and remains a valuable piece of history and Americana, members of his family attempted to suppress it, perhaps because he had, in some instances, too literally followed Samuel

Johnson's advice that if you are going to write a life, you must write it as it was.

He continued to write letters to the nation's newspapers and periodicals—among them the *Albany Sun*, the *North American Review*, the *New York Independent*. In 1887 he delivered the address for the class of 1832 before the alumni of Yale University. During these years, various reporters, historians, and students sought him out. They saw the old patriot's rich Bluegrass lands, the impressive mansion, and the stunning objets d'art gracing its white plaster walls and alcoves. "The hall is so large," wrote Frank G. Carpenter, "that you could turn a wagon load of hay about in it without touching the walls." Though General Clay was in his eighties, they found their host "almost as strong, intellectually and physically, as he was when he made his first abolition speech as a student in Yale . . . sixty years ago." His sagacity seemed unimpaired and his conversational powers brilliant.

In 1890 Clay addressed the Mexican War veterans of Ohio. He wrote on a wide range of subjects—from politics to agriculture and economics. He read a paper to the Filson Club called "Money." In many ways his shadow still fell ahead of the march of the American people. He denounced the corruption of the railroads and urged that they be nationalized. In the early 1890s he addressed the Maumee Historical Society at Put-in-Bay Island, Lake Erie, and he appeared before other regional and national groups.

But many of his old friends were dead now. Seward, his old enemy whom he was always proud of having survived in office, even under "Useless" Grant, as Clay termed him, was nearly two decades in his grave. His good friend and fellow emancipationist Salmon Chase had died as chief justice of the Supreme Court. His own son, Green Clay, who had lost his health in the war, fell seriously ill in 1883. The old general sadly watched his son's "slow descent into the unknown forever." Launey had regained his health, grown up, and was now gone from White Hall most of the time. He had married the beautiful Hattie Hardwick of Stanton, Kentucky. Mary Jane and the rest of Clay's family lived in their serene pride away from him.

Visiting with his tenants, Clay met the orphaned sister of his employee McClelland Richardson. Dora was only about fifteen years old, but she was attracted to the courtly general, as he to her. Announcement of their wedding plans in 1894 caused a local and national sensation. Characteristically, Cassius Clay rode roughshod over all obstacles to achieve his goal and took a schoolboyish delight in outwitting both his family and his enemies in the process. Although his relatives thought they had succeeded in preventing any person authorized to perform the marriage ceremony from doing so, under cover of night the wily Clay secured the services of the back-country minister Squire Isaac Newton Douglass and had him brought to White Hall, where he united the aging man and his youthful protégé.

All Kentucky was excited with the marriage between the famous octogenarian and a "child bride." Both the *Lexington Transcript* and the *Louisville Courier-Journal* carried front-page stories, as did newspapers throughout the nation. Under the bold heading, THE SAGE OF WHITE HALL, the *Courier-Journal* summarized the results of a reporter's interview: " VISIT TO GENERAL CASSIUS CLAY AT HIS BEAUTIFUL HOME. . . . A KENTUCKY WELCOME EXTENDED. . . . BRINGS OUT OLD BOURBON. . . . TELLS OF HIS MARRIAGE AND WHY HE MADE A FORT OF HIS RESIDENCE. . . . HIS MIND CLEAR AS A BELL AND HIS LOVE FOR HIS BRIDE FRESH AS A SCHOOL BOY'S."

Clay seemed to take a grim joy in emphasizing the qualities of White Hall as his castlekeep. The lime content of the mortar was high, he pointed out, "and it is so hard today that you cannot stick a knife-blade into it." He showed the interviewer one of the cannons with which he had defended the office of the *True American*. "You see it is made of brass. It is nearly three feet long and has a bore of one and a quarter inches. Now, suppose I was to shoot into a mob with that loaded with this new explosive, why it would tear them all to pieces. It would wipe them off the face of the earth."

Hoping for an interview and photograph, the reporter, who signed himself "B.T." in the *Transcript*, asked if he could see the young bride. "No," Clay replied, "she is not dressed to be seen. Her hair is not fixed in the fashionable way. You see she has no mother, nobody to fix her up like other girls are fixed." It would not be proper for her picture to be taken "until she is fixed up with nice clothes and her hair is properly dressed."

But the resourceful newspaperman did glimpse her long enough to note her "heavy suit of black hair." It was plaited and hung down her back to her waist. Dora was of medium height, and had intense black eyes set deep into her head. Her cheek bones were prominent, her mouth "fairly pretty." The sketch that had earlier appeared in many newspapers did not—in the reporter's judgment—even resemble her, much less do her justice.

The reporter concluded his article, "Some think the old General is crazy, but I do not think so." Perhaps, he ventured, the famed emancipationist was "in his second childhood," but "his mind is as clear as a bell. He is in excellent health, and bids to live many years if no accident should befall him."

When news of his marriage to Dora was bruited about the region, Judge John Cabell Chenault warned Clay that self-appointed guardians of the public morals in Richmond were fidgety about "the child bride." The judge, who had once been his friend, had not only refused to perform the ceremony, but also advised the general not to marry at all. There would be trouble, Clay had been told, possibly a "posse comitatus." The sequel has passed into a kind of twilight world between fact and fantasy.

Clay had dealt with mobs before, and he knew how to

deal with this one. He had carefully loaded his cannon with grapeshot mixed with nails and tacks, chiseled pieces of harrow spikes, jagged horseshoes, cut sections of trace chains, grated lead, and an assortment of nuts and bolts. The weapon was aimed directly at a huge dead water maple that stood within shouting distance from the mansion, slightly downhill by the side entrance gate.

A rain front had recently passed through central Kentucky, but the November weather had cleared and the air blew lightly through Clay's shaggy mane of hair and silvered beard. Dora stood at the upstairs boudoir window overlooking the piazza to the south.

Accounts of the incident vary, but at any rate Sheriff Josiah P. Simmons demanded that Clay surrender the girl, while the seven-man posse, seeing the feared cannon, sought protection behind the very maple tree and its dead limbs toward which Clay's weapon was trained.

"White Hall was built as a place of hospitality," he told the men. "It is through no fault of mine that I have been compelled to turn it into a fortress." His face darkened, and legend says the November day darkened with it. "But you have come upon these grounds without invitation. Brandishing weapons!" He looked up at the window where Dora stood, and announced that Mrs. Clay and he were legally married. He motioned toward the window, and they all saw her. "Now I have never in my life detained a woman against her will; and, by the same token, no one ever forced a woman from C. M. Clay either. If she wishes to leave me, she can tell you so herself." Dora shouted that she wanted to stay and take care of the general and White Hall. Clay bowed toward her slightly, then moved toward the cannon. "Now I admonish you, in the interest of peace, and salvation of life and limb, to leave these premises forthwith!"

With that warning, shots began to ring out. Clay fired his cannon and, scoring a direct hit, shattered the dead limbs of the water maple into splinters. The members of the posse retrieved their frightened horses and beat a hasty retreat up Clay Lane.*

Though the union created a national sensation and a local outrage, Clay declared, "I think she is a good, virtuous girl and I believe she will make me a good and loyal wife." His mellow smile and courtly demeanor took the edge off the complaints of self-righteous tongue-waggers and, in time, began to silence the would-be thieves of his happiness. Increasingly, people condoned his eccen-

---

* After a rest at Foxtown, the posse returned ingloriously to Richmond. There, according to William H. Townsend, *The Lion of White Hall* (Dunwoody, Ga.: Norman S. Berg, 1967, based on his recorded address of the same title at the Civil War Round Table, Chicago, Oct. 17, 1952), Simmons made his report to the county judge:

Richmond, Kentucky
November 14, 1894

Judge John C. Chenault, Dear Judge,
I am reportin' about the posse like you said I had to. Judge, we went out to White Hall but we didn't do no good. It was a mistake to go out there with only seven men. Judge, the general was awful mad. He got to cussin' and a shootin', and we had to shoot. I thought we hit him two or three times, but don't guess we did. He didn't act like it. We come out right good considerin'. I'm having some misery from two splinters of wood in my side. Dick [Colyer] was hurt a little when his shirt tail and britches was shot off by a piece of horseshoe and nails that come out of that old cannon. Have you seen Jack? [unidentified member of the posse] He wrenched his neck and shoulder when his horse throw'd him as we were gettin' away. Judge, I think you'll have to go to Frankfort and see Brown. [John Young Brown, who was the governor] If he could send Captain Longmire up here with two light fielders, he could divide his men, send some with the cannon around to the front of the house, not too close, and the others around through the corn field and up around the cabins and spring house to the back porch, I think this might do it. Respectfully,

Josiah P. Simmons, High sheriff.

131

tricities, and distinguished citizens once more sought his stirring eloquence at important events. During the twenty-ninth encampment of the Grand Army of the Republic at Phoenix Hill in Louisville, September 13, 1895, General Clay was the first speaker on the program; his topic was "Kentucky Soldiery." While in Louisville he was the house guest of Captain John Leathers, whose hospitable family provided him their best bedroom, and a bottle of Kentucky bourbon, purchased especially for the occasion, was placed on the chiffonier. When he was settled, they inquired if they could do anything else for him. The octogenarian bridegroom of less than a year courteously thanked them and replied that he would like, if possible, "the largest and finest doll in Louisville" to take back to White Hall for his new bride, Dora. After exhaustive shopping, Captain Leathers's daughter found such a doll–so large that they had to bring it home in a buggy. Upon leaving, General Clay thanked them for "the fine bottle of face lotion on the chiffonier." Then, as a granddaughter of Captain Leathers tells it, he took off "a beautiful ring–a large red stone with the double eagle insignia of the Romanoffs embedded in it," and presented it to Captain Leathers's daughter. The distinguished old general made a memorable picture driving off in a buggy with the large doll for his young bride at his side.

The marriage lasted about two years, after which Clay made the arrangements for Dora to move from White Hall to Valley View, where she had friends. He brought the divorce action himself and paid the costs. Although there was apparently no serious disagreement between them, the divorce was granted for separation. Wanting no doubts about his manhood to be raised, Clay declared that he had "fully met and discharged all the covenants of his marriage contract."

Soon thereafter Dora married Riley Brock, a handsome but shiftless young counterfeiter and moonshiner from the Kentucky River cliffs. Dora apparently persuaded the old general, who was as fond of her as ever, to take her back into White Hall as his housekeeper and to hire her husband as a tenant. In about one year, Dora gave birth to a son, whom she named Cassius Marcellus Clay Brock. About the relationship we cannot be sure, but the old general loved the little boy. Meanwhile, Riley Brock degenerated into a gambler, alcoholic, and general trouble-maker. In January 1900, Clay wrote an urgent note to his friend in Richmond, Dr. G. G. Perry:

Dear Dr.: Brock and Company have driven Dora crazy & taken her off with the sick baby.

They will return in force & rob my house—Help *me*—& *send Sant Oldham to* help *me.* Come *at* once."

C. M. Clay

Clay was waiting alone in front of the embers of his library fireplace when he heard the swollen windows being forced. Armed with pistol and bowie knife, he sought the shadows, ready once again to assert his right of self-defense. No one knows exactly what happened, but when help finally arrived from Richmond, General Clay was sitting in front of the fireplace, his robe singed and smoking from the battle. One of the men lay in a congealed pool of blood on the library floor, killed with Clay's pistol. In the morning light they found another one down behind the springhouse, stiff and cold, having received the death wound just below the navel. If the felons were indeed "Brock and Company," apparently Riley Brock and possibly one other confederate managed to elude Clay's knife and pistol and get away.

Clay was not seriously wounded, but he never seemed to rally to his old vigor after this fight. The mental decline, already begun, now mercilessly advanced. He became increasingly more unstable and suspicious. People on business, members of his family, and others were warned to approach White Hall only at the peril of their lives. In 1901 his refusal to pay taxes resulted in a second attempt to arrest Clay. "Why should I pay taxes?" he shouted from his castlekeep. "I get no protection." The sheriff left the subpoena, but the old man remained "barred up in his residence," so the official notation reads, "refusing admittance or to come out and be notified of my business with him."

Once he fired either his gun or his cannon—the account is vague—at an out-of-state visitor who wished to interview him. When the visitor returned to his hotel in Richmond, he was asked, "Did you get to talk to the Lion of White Hall?"

"No," he responded, "but I sure heard him roar!"

Clay bought Dora a little house in Woodford County and visited her occasionally, but he became increasingly isolated and eccentric. Fact gave way to gossip and tall tales. Whenever the older people told stories about his eloquent speeches, Clay was always "the Abolitionist."

Strange stories circulated among the credulous. Late at night the old general's lamp could be seen in windows of the many-roomed mansion. He went on nightly rambles, it was said, and talked with the illustrious dead. He argued with Henry Clay about freeing *his* slaves. He urged Lincoln to issue the Emancipation Proclamation. He had audiences with the Czar and Czarina of Russia. All their portraits hung on his walls. And there was his Russian mistress, the famed ballerina, who accounted for the strange music that emanated from the ballroom—the spirited mazurka and faint chords of the majestic quadrille. People said that Clay fought ghosts of his old enemies and slew them once again with his bowie knife. It was his penance for being an "autocrat of hell," Democrats said. Sometimes strange noises startled passersby in the dusk—sounds of old battles, cries of pain, and the roaring of a lion emerged from the cavernous hulk of White Hall. Venerable ex-slaves maintained with absolute conviction that the old lion not only conversed with the dead, but "scratched his head with lightning" and "purred himself to sleep at night with thunder."

By July 1903, news circulated throughout the Bluegrass that Cash Clay was dying of a kidney disease and an enlarged prostate gland. Across the world in the Vatican, Pope Leo XIII was also dying, and sporting central Kentuckians began to place their bets on who would live longer. "The Death Derby," they called it. Clay took a schoolboyish delight in not letting his supporters down. As weak as he was, so the story went, the old patriot remarked with a grim smile after the pope's death, "Well, I won, and I'm not even infallible."

Even the doctors, Tom and Waller Bullock, had difficulty getting inside White Hall to treat Clay, for he remained suspicious and belligerent when he did not recognize his callers. His temper flared out of control whenever he was irritated. His body servant reported an astonishing incident shortly before his death. On a hot summer day, Clay was obsessed with a large, bothersome fly—"my abomination," as he used to say. Bedfast, he propped himself up on the crutch of his rifle, took aim and pulled the trigger. Some plaster drifted down, but the fly was splattered over the ceiling.

On the night of July 22, 1903, his fiery spirit grew peaceful. His gnarled hands drew up the discolored sheets beneath his beard, and he slept. Outside, clouds scudded across the moon. The thick leaves of the stately trees around White Hall were troubled. The July air suddenly cooled and from the Cumberland Mountains to the south eerie sounds rolled over the muttering earth. Tempest-loving ravens scribed the hills and sought the shadows of the great eaves and fenestration hoods of the mansion. Trees shook like quivering reeds. The skies were riven in electric fire. Instantly, the roads between Richmond and Lexington became rivers. A mighty wind broke over the land, bending trees to the earth. Whole groves were dismantled and became piles of kindling wood. Barns were unroofed, and the church steeples of Richmond were torn off. Lightning tangled in tremulous skeins of rain. In Lexington, china shook in the closets, and a great thunderbolt struck off the head of the colossal Henry Clay monument and sent it two hundred feet down the flooded greensward.

Then, capriciously, the tornado ended. The clouds vanished as suddenly as they had come. The stars came out and silvered the Bluegrass landscape. In White Hall, the old general's body servant saw that his master was asleep. It was not a troubled sleep. Cassius Marcellus Clay was asleep for ever.

Addendum:
The Russian Ballerina

IN SPITE OF rich documentary sources, some areas of Clay's life remain a puzzle. The truth behind the Launey Clay adoption, for instance, has defied discovery by curious contemporaries and careful biographers alike. The isolated facts that I will treat here, considered together, may help us to define the problem, if not to solve it.

Mr. Floyd G. Clay kindly furnished me with a number of these facts in telephone conversations and in the personal interview he granted me May 23, 1974. Mr. Clay's father was Launey Clay, General Clay's adopted son. According to Madison County Courthouse records, he was born in Saint Petersburg, Russia, March 22, 1866, Old Style, and was originally named "Leonide Petroff." The adoption paper notes simply, "His father and mother Jean and Annie Petroff . . . put the said Leonide into the possession of " the petitioner, General Clay. The "Petition to Change Name" is dated August 11, 1873. On January 3, 1876, General Clay made a financial arrangement for Green Clay, in consideration of $2,000, to convey to Launey Clay an "undivided sixth interest" in the White Hall estate; in the event the boy died before the age of twenty-eight, the proceeds were to be paid "to the mother of Launey Clay[,] Annie Petroff[,] wife of Jean Petroff of St. Petersburg of the Empire of Russia during the natural life of said Annie Petroff." Launey Clay grew up and was educated in Madison County. Mr. Floyd Clay's mother was Launey Clay's first wife, the strikingly handsome

Hattie Hardwick of Stanton, Kentucky. When Floyd Clay was an infant, General Clay presented him with a personally inscribed photograph; he later gave Floyd Clay's grandfather Hardwick a handsomely engraved silver-banded powder horn. The boy was reared by his grandparents in Stanton after his parents were divorced.

Mr. Clay took exception to William H. Townsend's impression of his father, delivered in his Chicago Civil War Round Table Address (noted in "Sources and Acknowledgments")—especially the general impression Townsend conveyed that he was a "drifter." It was true, Mr. Clay stated, that Launey Clay as a young man had some alcoholic problems, but "he was a prohibitionist the last thirty years of his life." Further, his position as chemist for an ironworks took him to various parts of the country—Austin, Texas; Pueblo, Colorado; Goodrich, Tennessee; and towns throughout Ohio. During the latter part of his life he was a resident of Youngstown, Ohio, where he died of cancer December 14, 1933.

I reviewed the aging general's treatment of Launey, the legal arrangements he made on Launey's behalf, and his fierce loyalty to the boy in the face of self-appointed guardians of the public morals and tongue-wagging Victorians—and then asked Mr. Floyd Clay for his own explanation. He said with conviction: "I think he [Launey] was the son—*the blood son*—of General Clay. I've heard this all my life." This interview sheds a good deal of light upon the mystery and distortions in accounts of the life of Clay's Russian son. Compare, for example, the interview of Mrs. David Annabell Olson by Betty Cox, "Mrs. Olson remembers Clay and White Hall," in the *Madison County Newsweek*, March 16, 1974, in which Mrs. Olson is quoted as saying she was told about "a deathbed statement delivered by Cassius Clay to Mrs. [Lalla Rookh Fish Marsteller] Clay [the second wife of Clay's son Brutus]." The substance was that the son "who so many people said belonged to him was not of his blood," but was an offspring of a "beautiful Russian lady who was of the . . . royal family and not a ballerina with the Imperial Court Ballet, as believed by so many. Her name was Annie Petroff and it is allegedly her portrait that now hangs in the ballroom at White Hall." Supposedly, "the Russian woman sent her son to America to avoid the bloodshed she knew was sure to come with the approaching . . . Revolution."

Attorney Clay Shackelford, interviewed by me in Richmond, May 27, 1974, provided some information through his small but useful private collection of Clay letters, extending from Clay's New Haven days (1831) to the period of the Russian ministry at Saint Petersburg (1861–1869). A nephew of Miss Sally Keen Shackelford, Clay Shackelford lived next door to the so-called "Launey Clay house," at 814 West Main Street. Local stories persist that General Clay's Russian mistress lived there during the years after his return from Russia, that she spoke French, that the ladies of Richmond called her "the Countess," that they deliberately "picked up their skirts and crossed the street to avoid speaking to her," and that she eventually returned to Russia "because she found Madison County too tame." Another version holds that she later moved to Bourbon County, and still another that she lived in Florida for a time until General Clay invited her to Richmond, possibly waiting until his divorce from Mary Jane Clay was final (February 7, 1878).

But I could find no conclusive evidence that any of this was so. Nor could Mr. Shackelford verify any of these details. One of the most astonishing family stories dealt with General Green Clay. When he was but "a 17-year-old boy attending William and Mary College" (about 1774), he joined a surveying party sponsored by Judge Richard Henderson of North Carolina, and "posed as an illiterate—general handyman and pot-walloper." Then in the evenings, while the surveyors went over their records, he lay awake listening and copied them down. Later, he beat them back to the land office to file his claims. And that was how he came into possession of a good part of his huge landholdings. Whether true or not, it is a fascinating addendum to Lewis Collins's *Historical Sketches of Kentucky* (Cincinnati: J. A. & U. P. James, 1847, pp. 243–45).

Of the many valuable letters bearing on Clay's life in the Cassius M. Clay Collection at Lincoln Memorial University, Harrogate, Tennessee, one of the most puzzling is a letter in French from "Count Tolstoy," dated 25 September 1863, the substance of which indicates that in July 1863, just over two months after the American minister's return trip to Russia, Clay had indicated a desire to place into "la Salle d'asyle du Prince [d'Oldenbourg]" a child, referred to by Tolstoy as "le fils de Votre chasseur" (the son of your footman), the payment being ninety silver rubles for the first year, seventy-five for each succeeding year. Of special relevance here may be the portion of the *Memoirs* (pp. 343–45) concerning both the ballet and "asylums for infants." The cost of Clay's sponsorship of the child, perhaps the equivalent of between one and two thousand dollars annually today, bespeaks a strong personal interest of some kind. Certain it is that more modest social and financial arrangements could have been made if the child was, indeed, that of his footman. One speculates that the child may have been Clay's own. If so, the date of 1866, which he gives as the birthdate of the child he adopted in Russia, "Leonide Petroff," may suggest inconsistency, although possible explanations are abundant. It may not be without some future relevance to note here his footman's name—rendered "John" in English, "Jean" in French. As of this writing, I have not yet found a record of his footman's surname.

Mrs. Ezekiel Field Clay, in a letter to me dated April 14, 1974, from Paris, Kentucky, confirmed the possible authenticity of the oil portrait—purportedly that of Anna Petroff—which hangs in the ballroom of White Hall. She wrote that after General Clay's death her husband's father "went to White Hall and bought it and brought it to Paris." This information is supported by the Madison County courthouse records. The administrator of Cassius

M. Clay's estate, the State Bank and Trust Company in Richmond, placed all his personal possessions on the auction block October 8, 1903. According to the "Report of Sale" of that day, several oil paintings sold. However, the one purchased by "E. F. Clay, Jr.," without description, sold for $100, a sum higher than any other portrait brought, even those of the "Emperor and Empress of Russia," which together brought only $38 (pp. 15, 10). This is the *only* purchase that Ezekiel Field Clay, Jr., made, although literally hundreds of items, many of them valuable objets d'art, went under the hammer. According to the family understanding, the portrait was sent to General Clay by Czar Alexander II upon his return to America from his Russian mission, which would be during or subsequent to the late fall of 1869.

Local legend says that General Clay kept this portrait in the small anteroom to the left of the main entrance hall and that he rarely allowed anyone to see it. One interesting sidelight from the Ezekiel Field Clays is that after its purchase, the portrait was stored in the attic for many years, that it was moved and in the process somehow was dropped from a window. This is one explanation of its being newly restored. Upon observing a photograph of the pose—the tantalizing raising of the right hand, the beckoning eyes, the three-quarter view of the half-nude, "suggesting a woodland nymph"—Mr. Addison Franklin Page, director and curator of the J. B. Speed Art Museum, Louisville, Kentucky told me in an interview, June 25, 1974, that the work "could be a portrait of that period." He observed that "the gesture, calculated to heighten intimacy, was conventional," and that the "way of dressing the hair was fashionable in the style of the time." He agreed, too, that a ballerina of the Maryinsky Theatre could possibly have posed for it; and that it was much more likely that she would pose for it than a grand duchess, a princess, a countess, or a member of the Romanoff family—at least, an openly acknowledged member. He added some interesting information about the long tradition of "beautiful and enormously talented Russian serfs of the period."

Among the most fascinating of the materials in the William H. Townsend collection, now in the possession of Mrs. Townsend and her daughter, Mrs. Mary Genevieve Murphy, are the two personal photograph albums that belonged to General Clay. There are only two photographs of ballet dancers, and they are of the same ballerina. Her name is Marie Petipa, or, more accurately, Marie Surovschikova Petipa. They are both photographic *cartes de visite*. The first, depicting her in the classical white ballet costume of the 1860s, bears the inscription in Clay's hand, "given me by her March 11, 1865." In the second, arms akimbo, head up, and eyes directly at the lens, she strikes the proud pose of a Cossack, complete with boots, tunic, sash, and a dark headband tilted over her forehead; this photograph bears Clay's notation, "given me by her May 1, 1865."

Concerning Surovschikova (her patronymic name was Sergeevna, for Serge), as she was known before she married choreographer-director Marius Ivanovich Petipa in 1854, Serge Lifar, in his *History of Russian Ballet from Its Origins to the Present Day*, trans. Arnold Haskell (New York: Roy Publishers, n.d), writes, "Finally, after 1860, Europe discovered two more great Russian stars: Petipa-Sourovstchikova [*sic*] and M[arfa] Mouraviova" (p. 10). And on page 105: "One of the *premiers sujets* of Marius Petipa, along with Sokolova, Amossova, and Radina, Sourovtchikova was his favourite, whom he was later [1854] to marry." According to Petipa, she was "the most graceful of all dancers, with the body of a Venus."

Her career was a strange one. She left the Imperial School in 1854, but she had been dancing for long before and was already known as a coming star. Her marriage with Petipa was of double value: to begin with the choreographer set to work with added keenness, anxious to make a world-wide star of his wife; and on

142

the other hand her position as Marius Petipa's wife opened every door—and every stage—to her.

On her side Sourovtchikova had a great influence on her husband, and through him on the destiny of Russian ballet. Marius Petipa strove to compose works which were perfectly suited to his wife's talent and personality, ballets such as *The Paris Market, The Blue Dahlia, Marriage under the Regency, The Dancer Abroad, The Belle of Lebanon, Florida*, etc.

Sourovtchikova, now famous, danced abroad [as well as in Saint Petersburg] after 1861 (particularly in Paris, Berlin, and Riga), where her character dances were a sensation—she was especially good in the kazatchok and the mazurka. Her standing grew from day to day. . . . But her career came to an end . . . . she separated from Petipa in 1867, and lost her position in 1869. [P. 105]

A footnote in Marius Petipa's *Memoirs* (published as *Russian Ballet Master: The Memoirs of Marius Petipa*, ed. Lillian Moore, trans. Helen Whittaker [New York: Macmillan, 1958]) states that Marie Sergeevna Surovschikova was a graduate of the Imperial Ballet School of Saint Petersburg in 1854; she was "svelte, slender, with slim ankles and arrow-like points," having little in common with the typical buxom, sturdy ballerinas of the 1860s. She possessed an "extraordinary flair for mime and *demi-charactère* dancing, which enabled her to shine in a wide variety of roles in spite of the fragility which prevented her from mastering spectacular *tours de force*." According to the information in the note, she was born in 1836 (she would have been about 29 when she gave her *cartes de visite* to Clay), and died in 1882; however Petipa presents an ambiguity when he states (on p. 58), "My first wife died in Piatigorsk in 1875."

An examination of the photographs of Marie (Surovschikova) Petipa in Clay's personal albums and the portrait of the seminude figure which hangs in White Hall, purportedly that of Anna Petroff, reveals a number of striking similarities—enough that pictorial evidence points to the possibility that the portrait is that of Surovschikova-Petipa, the famed ballerina of the magnificent flowering of classic Russian ballet in the third quarter of the nineteenth century.

Assuming this possibility, was the lady then Clay's mistress? If so, was she the mother of Launey (Leonide Petroff) Clay? We cannot now make a final judgment, but affirmative answers to each of these questions seem within the realm of possibility. The birth of Leonide Petroff, on March 22, 1866, followed the first *carte de visite* by precisely one year and the second by approximately 10½ months. Moreover there exists, in my judgment, a close resemblance between the physiognomies of Launey Clay at about age twelve and Marie Surovschikova Petipa, especially as seen in the photograph of May 1, 1865 (compare such features as the eyes, jaw lines, and chins).

But why do the adoption papers specify the names of the parents of Leonide Petroff as Jean and Annie Petroff? No fully satisfactory answer can yet be given. However, Clay states in his *Memoirs* that he "sent for my adopted son, Launey Clay, from Russia and . . . by permission of his *nominal* parents, assumed his guardianship" (p. 543, italics added). Concerning the conveyance of an undivided sixth interest in the White Hall estate, January 3, 1876, Clay specified that if the boy died before the age of twenty-eight, the proceeds were to go "to the mother of Launey Clay[,] Annie Petroff[,] wife of Jean Petroff of St. Petersburg of the Empire of Russia during the natural life of said Annie Petroff." Would Clay have provided so liberally for "nominal" parents? Perhaps so, as a consideration for their early care of the child, but the possibility that the name Petroff, a common one in Russia, was assumed for any number of reasons, including a remarriage, should not be overlooked.

Pursuing the hypothesis further, after a meteoric rise to world fame, Surovschikova's career, as Serge Lifar points out, was "a strange one." By 1867, the year following

Launey Clay's birth, she and the "official deputy ballet-master," Marius Ivanovich ("Jean" in French, "John" in English) Petipa, were divorced; and by 1869, the year Clay left Russia, Surovschikova "lost her position." Except for her death, noted in Marius Petipa's *Memoirs* as 1882 (or, ambiguously, in "Piatigorsk in 1875"), we do not hear from her again. It may not be insignificant to note, however, that when Clay wrote his *Memoirs*, working so diligently by 1884 that he was "forced to brevity in all other work," he rhapsodically soliloquized upon "that one image—that one voice which for so many years in a strange land I had listened to as the sweetest music . . . till in my dreams I saw the imploring looks, and heard the calling for me of the lost one." Then in reference to the birth of the male child in 1866, he declared, "To the secret of his parentage I am the only living witness— I who have, of all men living, the best reason to know" (p. 555). The inference seems clear enough: by 1884 the natural mother of Launey Clay was dead.

Finally, when William H. Townsend referred to Clay's mistress as the ballerina "Anna Jean Petroff," he was, perhaps, combining the names of the "nominal parents" mentioned in the deed of conveyance of 1876. Other than in the sources previously noted, I have been unable to find any other references to Anna and Jean Petroff, nor to any ballerina with the name Anna Jean Petroff. Lifar notes an "A. Petrov" danced *Le Pavillon d'Armide* May 19, 1909 (p. 230), and Galina and Moussia Petrov are mentioned among rising stars of the twentieth century (p. 227), but all three are too late, of course, to have known Clay intimately in the 1860s.

A Note on Sources and Acknowledgments

MUCH INFORMATION on Cassius Marcellus Clay has been gleaned from conversations, interviews, correspondence, and private collections of manuscripts, letters, records, paintings and photographs, and other memorabilia. In order to mention them here at all, I am obliged to combine the customary formal recognition of sources with the more personal courtesies of acknowledgment.

Although my interest in Clay dates back to the 1930s, more specifically this book began with the recent completion of a manuscript for a novel inspired by Clay's extraordinary life. I began that project about eight years ago, first working alone and then in collaboration with Frederick B. Shroyer, of Monterey Park, California. The research attendant to the novel inevitably provided general background information as well as an incentive for this book.

The major primary sources are Clay's own writings, especially *The Life of Cassius Marcellus Clay: Memoirs, Writings, and Speeches*, vol. 1 (Cincinnati: J. Fletcher Brennan & Company, 1886); *The Writings of Cassius Marcellus Clay (including Speeches and Addresses)*, ed. Horace Greeley (New York: Harper & Brothers, 1848); and numerous uncollected addresses and writings, such as his *Speech . . . before the Law Department of the University of Albany*, Albany, New York, February 3, 1863 (New York: Wynkoop, Hallenbeck & Thomas, 1863); his *Address . . . before the Alumni of Yale Univer-*

sity, [New Haven, Conn.], June 28, 1887 (published in the *New York Times*, June 29, 1887); and his controversial *Oration . . . before the Students and Historical Class of Berea College*, Berea, Kentucky, October 16, 1895 (published Richmond, Kentucky, 1895)—among hundreds of other speeches, letters, and papers.

All his life Clay was the kind of personality who made news—sometimes sensational news—so it is hardly surprising that innumerable contemporary accounts appear in pamphlets, books, magazines, and newspapers. Among the most valuable files are those of the *Observer and Reporter, Intelligencer, Morning Transcript*, and *Morning Herald*, all published in Lexington, Kentucky; the *Register* and *Climax* of Richmond; the *Journal, Examiner*, and *Courier-Journal* of Louisville; the *Democrat* and *Messenger* of Saint Louis; the *Cincinnati Gazette;* the important antislavery journal *National Era* (Washington, D.C.); *Niles' Weekly Register* (76 vols., 1811–1849); William Lloyd Garrison's *Liberator* (1831–1865); the *Philadelphia Record;* the *Evening Post,* the *World,* and the antislavery *Times* of New York; and even the *Daily News* and *Times* of London.

The letters from Clay's contemporaries—among them Abraham Lincoln, Salmon Chase, Charles A. Dana, Joshua Giddings, Chancellor Alexander M. Gortchacow, Frederick Douglass, Horace Greeley, George W. Julian, John M. Harlan, Wendell Phillips, William H. Seward, Edwin Stanton, Harriet Beecher Stowe, Fanny Kemble, and the ladies of the Ashtabula County (Ohio) Anti-Slavery Society—provide insight into the many facets of Clay's achievements and personality. Several of the most pertinent of these letters Clay included in his *Memoirs,* and most of the others can be found in the Cassius M. Clay Collection at Lincoln Memorial University, along with a mass of his Russian correspondence. Letters from Clay to Chase, Giddings, Julian, Stanton, and Douglass are in the Library of Congress manuscripts collection, Washington, D.C. Early accounts of the great events in which Clay participated can be found in such sources as Murat Halstead's *A History of the National Political Conventions* (Columbus, O.: Follett, Foster & Co., 1860), Asa Earl Martin's *The Anti-Slavery Movement in Kentucky, Prior to 1850* (Louisville: Filson Club, 1918), and Allen T. Rice's *Reminiscences of Abraham Lincoln* (New York: North American Publishing Co., 1886).

Legal documents and records of the county and circuit courts in the Madison and Fayette County courthouses have been absolutely essential in establishing and clarifying certain facts. The staff of the White Hall State Shrine, especially Director Jouette "Bucky" Walters, former director Edgar G. Archer, and Joy Jones Henderson, have been most helpful in providing detailed information. Very useful are the many collections of Clay and Clay-related materials in various institutions, among them the Filson Club, Louisville; the libraries of the University of Louisville, the University of Kentucky, and Berea College; the Louisville and Lexington public libraries; the State Archives of Frankfort, Ky.; the Kentucky Historical Society; and the Rare Book Room of the Huntington Library, San Marino, California.

The Brutus J. Clay letters, records, manuscripts, and artifacts in the private collection of R. Berle Clay at Auvergne, Paris, Kentucky, have been indispensable. I am indebted to him for arranging three full days during which I examined a portion of these materials. In addition to revealing letters exchanged between the two brothers, General Green Clay's library and some of his eighteenth-century writings are preserved, along with all the plantation records of Auvergne from 1837 onward. Most pertinent to this work, the revised *Memoirs* (vol. 1) and *Writings* (which Clay apparently planned to republish as vol. 2) are retained along with revisions and insertions, many written in Clay's own hand, interleaved supplements, rare clippings, emendations, and comments of Clay's proposed editor and literary executor, Henry Clay Howard. Although I have drawn upon this source to a substantial extent, I wish to emphasize here the larger importance of the entire collection as a future reservoir for agronomists as well as historians and students of American culture.

The William H. Townsend collection of Clay materials, including the Clay photograph albums, the "dress-up" bowie knife, Mr. Townsend's important notes on Clay, and other memorabilia, is another valuable source of information. I wish to express my gratitude to Mrs. Townsend and her daughter, Mrs. Mary Genevieve Murphy, and to Mr. Joe H. Murphy, Jr., for arranging for me to see these materials and for permitting me to use the Dora Richardson Clay portrait, photographs of the Clay children, the Marie Petipa *cartes de viste*, and other Townsend materials in this book.

I wish to acknowledge the cooperation and assistance of Dr. Frank W. Welch, president of Lincoln Memorial University, and Dr. Joseph E. Suppiger, chairman of the Department of History there, who provided me access to the absolutely essential Cassius M. Clay Collection at Harrogate, Tennessee. Special thanks are due Dr. Suppiger and Lincoln Memorial University photographer Rick Cary for the excellent reproduction of the photograph of Clay in the uniform of a Major General of Volunteers (ca. 1862); professionals James W. Todd, James M. Cox, and Jimmy Taylor of Richmond for their skilled photographic contributions to this work; Mr. and Mrs. Floyd G. Clay of Lexington for their kind permission to use the 1858 ambrotype of Brutus J. Clay; Suzanne Mitchell of the fine arts department of the University of Louisville for painstaking reproduction of the ambrotype; and Ron Cianciulli, her able student, for further photographic work of high quality.

Special thanks are due John T. Demos, director of libraries, University of Louisville, and his cooperative staff for their thoroughgoing efforts in obtaining necessary research materials and often providing reproduction services; and to the then dean of the Graduate School,

John A. Dillon, Jr., for arranging from limited monies a modest grant from the Graduate School Projects Fund, which allayed some of the expenses during the early stages of my research. I am especially grateful to Miss Genevieve Oswald, curator of the Dance Collection, the New York Public Library, for information on the life of Marie S. Petipa and her arrangement for and permission to use photoreproductions of the ballerina, a part of the rich special collection which she has done so much to assemble.

Mr. Ernest E. Weyhrauch, director of libraries, and Mrs. Sharon McConnell, curator of the John Wilson Townsend Collection at Eastern Kentucky University, Richmond, have been most helpful in arranging access to such useful materials as Clay's *Writings* (1848) and the unpublished 234-page manuscript compiled by Green Clay Herrick, son of Mary Barr Clay and nephew of General Clay. Having spent much of his life in Richmond and at White Hall, some of the author's insights into the life and personality of his uncle, whom he vividly remembered, are invaluable. One anecdote is representative. Always a moderate user of whiskey, though a lavish entertainer, General Clay kept several barrels of choice stock in his basement for aging; often he used it as a face lotion and body liniment. When he caught several of his young nephews in a tipsy state after they had slipped down into the spacious cellar and imbibed freely, he locked them up for about five hours, "until they were sober enough to climb back up stairs" (p. 232). The papers of Green Clay Herrick are now in the possession of Judge Watson Clay of Frankfort, Kentucky, to whom I am obliged for permitting me to reproduce those most pertinent to my research, and for allowing me to photocopy and use his early portraits of Cassius M. Clay and Maria Barr Warfield. I wish to thank Mr. George Haw of Richmond, Virginia, for providing information on his grandmother, Anne Warfield Clay Crenshaw, and for offering to arrange access to the fascinating Clay family lore of his aunt, Miss Fanny Graves Crenshaw.

Numerous short articles and pamphlets on Clay's time and culture are available, but the most generally known treatment is William H. Townsend's *The Lion of White Hall* (Dunwoody, Ga.: Norman S. Berg, 1967, based on his recorded address of the same title at the Civil War Round Table, Chicago, Oct. 17, 1952); the booklet is riddled with errors and misspellings, although the author was not responsible for the publisher's errata. Townsend here concentrates on the personality of Clay, and the picture he paints is dramatic, drawing on a wide range of local sources that would not otherwise be available today. The work is hardly a life, but rather an impression, frankly and primarily old-fashioned Kentucky oratory at its best; *The Lion of White Hall* was never intended to possess a finished historical balance. The letter of High Sheriff Josiah Simmons, as well as the *posse-comitatus* incident and Clay's last fight, appears in both the speech and the booklet, and I wish to acknowledge Townsend as source. Apocryphal though his version may seem, ample references to Clay's violent encounter with the law exist in courthouse documents and newspaper accounts. See, for example, the stories in the *Lexington Morning Herald*, April 6, 1901, headlined "GEN. CLAY FIRED ON OFFICERS," with the captions, "Believed They Were Spies, Many Shots Exchanged," "Vendetta," "The Fire Returned," and "Officers Retired"; on April 7, 1901, the headline "IS AT WAR WITH WORLD," is followed by "General Clay Barricaded and Threatens to Kill Intruders," "He Was Not Wounded," and "The Deadline"; and on page 3 of the same edition, "THE WRIT WITHDRAWN." Howard L. Colyer, nephew of Hugh H. Colyer, indicates that Townsend's name "Dick Collier" is in error, and should read "Hugh Colyer"; however, he confirms the widely held view that General Clay did, indeed, fire his cannon at a posse (interview, Richmond, Ky., May 27, 1974). Clay's letter of distress to Dr. G. G. Perry is in the Townsend collection. I am further indebted to Townsend for other general information, such as Clay's difficulty with jealous Russian noblemen and his affair with the ballerina, whom he designates as "Anna Jean Petroff" (see "Addendum: The Russian Ballerina" above).

I cannot let this opportunity pass without emphasizing the fact that it was William H. Townsend who first brought Cassius Marcellus Clay into prominence as an American hero and, as early as the 1920s, did the pioneering research that has led to the more widely ranging interest, historical and otherwise, in his life today.

The only book-length biography, David L. Smiley's *Lion of White Hall: The Life of Cassius M. Clay* (Madison: University of Wisconsin Press, 1962), presents a useful assemblage of source materials on Clay's political career but is weak in depicting the personality of Clay—his force of character, his turbulent spirit, those spicy ingredients that have made him a living legend.

William H. Townsend's *Lincoln and His Wife's Home Town* (Indianapolis, Ind.: Bobbs-Merrill, 1929) is as historically thorough as his famous speech and pamphlet *The Lion of White Hall* is factually free-wheeling; yet it gives us almost as much information on Cassius Clay as on Abraham Lincoln and suggests subtle depths of Clay's influence upon his president that most other historians have missed or failed to treat. Thomas D. Clark's chapter, "Lion of White Hall," in *The Kentucky* (New York: Farrar and Rinehart, 1942) is an introductory sketch of Clay's life and my source for the "Bull's Hell" story.

Good general references on the Civil War and Reconstruction period include such books as J. G. Jarrell and David Donald, *The Civil War and Reconstruction* (Lexington, Mass.: D. C. Heath, 1969), which provides insights on the old-line Whig scalawag–Negro alliance during Reconstruction, and Avery Craven, *Reconstruction: The Ending of the Civil War* (New York: Holt, Rinehart and Winston, 1969), in which the scalawag with the "Old Whig spirit" is quoted, with credit given to Donald's earlier article "The Scalawag in Mississippi Reconstruction," *Journal of Southern History* 10 (1944): 447–60. Hans L. Trefousse, *The Radical Republicans: Lincoln's Vanguard for Racial Justice* (New York: Alfred A. Knopf, 1969) supersedes all other work in this field. For Reconstruction politics, see Lawanda Cox and John H. Cox, *Politics, Principle, and Prejudice, 1865–1866* (London: Free Press of Glencoe, Collier-Macmillan, 1963) and Eric L. McKitrick, *Andrew Johnson and Reconstruction* (Chicago: University of Chicago Press, 1960). Among other works shedding light on the time, culture, and events of Clay's life are these: J. Winston Coleman, Jr., *Slavery Times in Kentucky* (New York: Johnson Reprint Corp., 1970, originally published by the University of North Carolina Press, 1940), and his pamphlet *Last Days, Death and Funeral of Henry Clay* (Lexington, Ky.: Winburn Press, 1951), which mentions the tornado that swept the Bluegrass the night of Cassius Clay's death; Jean M. Howard, "The Ante-Bellum Career of Cassius Marcellus Clay," M.A. thesis, University of Kentucky, 1947; Jay Monaghan, *Diplomat in Carpet Slippers* (Indianapolis, Ind.: Bobbs-Merrill Co., 1947), a secondary source for Clay's encounter with the *duellistes* in the Saint Petersburg restaurant; and James Rood Robertson, *A Kentuckian at the Court of the Tsars: The Ministry of Cassius Marcellus Clay to Russia* (Berea, Ky.: Berea College Press, 1935), a labor of love in its authoritative assemblage of details on Clay's Russian mission, but sketchy on personality.

It is impossible to mention the names of all who have contributed to this book, but I wish especially to thank Mrs. Alice Preston Luckett and Mr. Frank G. Rankin, the program chairman of the Louisville Civil War Round Table who interviewed her, March 10, 1974 and provided me with the doll story. Modest local histories such as

Jonathan Truman Dorris and Maud Weaver Dorris, *Glimpses of Historic Madison County, Kentucky* (Nashville, Tenn.: Williams Co., 1955) provide essential facts and historical observations that otherwise would have been carried away in the flood of larger issues. Coleman's *Famous Kentucky Duels* (Lexington, Ky.: Henry Clay Press, 1969) and *The Squire's Sketches of Lexington* (Lexington, Ky.: Henry Clay Press, 1972) are small mines yielding some surprising finds. I am grateful to "Squire" J. Winston Coleman, Jr., for his advice, for the opportunity to examine his impressive Kentuckiana collection, and specifically for his kind permission to include the prints made from glass negatives of White Hall and General Clay, originally taken by Lexington photographer Isaac C. Jenks, November 13, 1894, on the old lion's second wedding day.